GCSE History is always topical with CGP...

If you're studying "Crime and Punishment in Britain c1000-Present" for Edexcel GCSE History, this CGP Topic Guide will keep you on the straight and narrow...

It's packed with crystal-clear revision notes for the whole topic, plus plenty of helpful activities, sample answers, exam tips, exam-style questions and more. It's a steal!

How to access your free Online Edition

This book includes a free Online Edition to read on your PC, Mac or tablet.
To access it, just go to **cgpbooks.co.uk/extras** and enter this code...

3995 0696 5546 7470

By the way, this code only works for one person. If somebody else has used this book before you, they might have already claimed the Online Edition.

CGP — still the best! ☺

Our sole aim here at CGP is to produce the highest quality books — carefully written, immaculately presented and dangerously close to being funny.

Then we work our socks off to get them out to you — at the cheapest possible prices.

Published by CGP

Editors:
Izzy Bowen, Andy Cashmore, Emma Cleasby, Robbie Driscoll, Sophie Herring, Kathryn Kaiser and Jack Tooth.

Contributors:
Ben Armstrong, Paddy Gannon and Paul Smith.

With thanks to Sophie Herring, Catherine Heygate, Katya Parkes and Helen Tanner for the proofreading.
With thanks to Emily Smith for the copyright research.

Acknowledgements:
Cover image: LONDON: CHILDREN'S PRISON Boys exercising at Tothill Fields Prison. Wood engraving, 1861, from Henry Mayhew's London Labour and the London Poor. / Granger / Bridgeman Images
With thanks to Alamy for permission to use the images on pages 5, 12, 28, 46, 48, 54, 64, 72, 74, 79 and 86.
With thanks to Mary Evans for permission to use the images on pages 8, 10, 14, 18, 26, 34, 38, 75 and 82.
Image used on page 40: Petition by Trade Unionists to the King in Copenhagen Fields, 21st April 1834, engraved by W.Summers, 1836 / London Metropolitan Archives, City of London / Bridgeman Images.
With thanks to Getty Images for permission to use the images on pages 60 and 88.
Image used on page 81: Notice issued by the Metropolitan Police regarding Jack the Ripper, 30 September 1888 (engraving), English School, (19th century) / Private Collection / Look and Learn / Peter Jackson Collection / Bridgeman Images.
Police letter (1888) from Charles Warren to Percy Lindley used on page 89 from The National Archives, transcript reference MEPO 1/ 48 contains public sector information licensed under the Open Government Licence v3.0. http://www.nationalarchives.gov.uk/doc/open-government-licence/version/3/

Contents

Exam Hints and Tips

You'll have to take three papers in Edexcel GCSE History. This book will help you to prepare for Paper 1.

You will take 3 Papers altogether

1) Paper 1 is 1 hour 15 minutes long. It's worth 52 marks — 30% of your GCSE. This paper will be divided into two sections:
- Section A: Historic Environment.
- Section B: Thematic Study.

> This book covers the Thematic Study Crime and Punishment in Britain, c.1000-present and the Historic Environment Whitechapel, c.1870-c.1900.

2) Paper 2 is 1 hour 45 minutes long. It's worth 64 marks — 40% of your GCSE. This paper will be divided into two question and answer booklets:
- Booklet P: Period Study.
- Booklet B: British Depth Study.

> It's really important that you make sure you know which topics you're studying for each paper.

3) Paper 3 is 1 hour 20 minutes long. It's worth 52 marks — 30% of your GCSE. This paper will be divided into two sections, both about a Modern Depth Study:
- Section A: two questions, one of which is source-based.
- Section B: A four-part question based on 2 sources and 2 interpretations.

Remember these Tips for Approaching the Questions

Organise your Time in the exam

1) The more marks a question is worth, the longer your answer should be.
2) Don't get carried away writing loads for a question that's only worth four marks — you'll need to leave time for the higher mark questions.

> Try to leave a few minutes at the end of the exam to go back and read over your answers.

Always use a Clear Writing Style

1) It's a good idea to start essay answers with a brief introduction and end with a conclusion.
2) Remember to start a new paragraph for each new point you want to discuss.
3) Try to use clear handwriting and pay attention to spelling, grammar and punctuation. In the 16-mark question, there are an extra four marks available for SPaG.

Plan your essay answers

1) For longer essay questions, it's important to make a quick plan before you start writing.
2) Think about what the key words are in the question. Scribble a quick plan of your main points — cross through this neatly at the end so it isn't marked.

> You don't need to plan answers for the shorter questions.

Stay Focused on the question

1) Make sure that you answer the question. Don't just chuck in everything you know about the topic.
2) You've got to be accurate — make sure you include precise details like the names and dates of important laws and acts.

> It might help to write the first sentence of every paragraph in a way that addresses the question, e.g. "Another reason why crime changed in the medieval period was..."

Skills for the Thematic Study

The main part of <u>Paper 1</u> is the <u>Thematic Study</u>. There are three questions which test <u>two main skills</u>.

There are Three types of exam question in the Thematic Study

1) In the first question, you'll need to <u>compare two</u> different <u>time periods</u>. You'll be asked about a <u>similarity</u> or <u>difference</u> between these two periods, and will need to explain your answer.

> Explain one way that prisons in the period c.1700-c.1900 were different from those in the period c.1900-present. [4 marks]

2) The next question will ask you to <u>explain</u> something about a change — e.g. <u>why</u> something changed over a certain time, or why changes were <u>slow</u> / <u>quick</u> to happen. Make sure you <u>analyse</u> each point fully, including plenty of <u>detail</u>.

> Explain why witchcraft laws changed in the period c.1500-c.1700. [12 marks]

3) The final task will cover at least <u>200 years</u> of history. You'll get a choice of two questions — answer the one you're most <u>comfortable</u> with. Each one will give a <u>statement</u> and you'll be asked how <u>far you agree</u> with it.

> 'The nature of punishment was transformed in the period c.1700-present day.' Explain how far you agree. [16 marks]

4) Decide your opinion <u>before</u> you begin writing, state it clearly at the start and end of your answer, and include evidence for <u>both sides</u> of the argument.

> There are also 4 marks available for spelling, punctuation, grammar and the use of specialist terminology in the final task, so it's worth 20 marks in total.

In question types 2) and 3), you'll be given two '<u>stimulus points</u>' (hints about things you could include in your answer). You don't <u>have</u> to include them, so <u>don't panic</u> if you can't remember much about them. But you <u>must</u> always give <u>other information</u> to get full marks.

The thematic study tests Two Main Skills

Knowledge and Understanding

1) For <u>all the thematic study questions</u>, you'll get marks for showing <u>knowledge and understanding</u> of the <u>key features</u> of the topic.

2) You'll need to use <u>accurate</u> and <u>relevant</u> information to <u>explain changes</u> in different historical periods. You'll also need to use <u>evidence</u> to <u>support</u> your answers to the longer essay questions.

> The <u>Knowledge and Understanding</u> activities in this book will help you to revise the <u>important facts</u> for each period so that you have <u>plenty of information</u> to help you in the exam.

Thinking Historically

1) The thematic study is divided into <u>four</u> different <u>time periods</u>, but you'll need to think about the topic as a <u>whole</u> for the exam and make <u>links</u> between different periods.

2) The study focuses on what <u>changed</u> (and <u>what didn't change</u>) over time and <u>why</u>. The questions will ask you about historical concepts like <u>continuity</u>, <u>change</u>, <u>similarity</u> and <u>difference</u>. You'll also need to know the <u>main factors</u> that caused or prevented change — things like <u>social changes</u>, <u>technology</u> and <u>attitudes</u>.

> The <u>Thinking Historically</u> activities will get you thinking about the <u>significance</u> of <u>different factors</u>, <u>turning points</u> in crime and punishment and how much <u>change</u> or <u>continuity</u> there has been across different periods in history.

The Thematic Study is all about change over time...

The Thematic Study appears a bit daunting because it covers such a long period of time but don't worry — in this book the topic is broken down into different time periods to help you.

Skills for the Historic Environment

These two pages will help you understand the Historic Environment section of the exam. There are two main skills you'll need — a good knowledge of Whitechapel and the ability to use sources.

You'll need to Write About the Key Features of Whitechapel

1) In the Historic Environment section of the exam, you'll be expected to show your knowledge and understanding of crime in Whitechapel, as well as your ability to analyse sources.

2) The activities in the Historic Environment section of this book will help you to practise the skills you'll need for the exam.

Knowledge and Understanding

1) In the Historic Environment section, you'll need to be able to identify and talk about the key features of your site — in this case, Whitechapel.

2) Question 1 will ask you to describe two different features of a certain aspect of Whitechapel.

3) To get all four marks, you'll need to identify two features and then give a little bit of extra information that's relevant to each one.

> Key features of a historical site are any details, characteristics or unique features that stand out and make the site, or part of it, special. They are the main or most important characteristics of the site. For example, poor living conditions, high levels of immigration, and high crime rates are all key features of Whitechapel.

> Give a description of **two** features of the Whitechapel Vigilance Committee.   [4 marks]

> You only need to talk about two key features — writing about more won't get you extra marks.

> Identify a feature, then add some supporting information that gives a bit more detail.

> The Whitechapel Vigilance Committee was made up of local people who wanted to catch Jack the Ripper. The Committee organised street patrols and hired private detectives to look into the case.
> The Committee caused problems for police detectives who were investigating the Ripper murders. The police wasted time looking into leads identified by the Committee that turned out to be false.

> Make sure your supporting information is linked to the feature that you've talked about.

4) To answer Question 1, you'll need to have a good knowledge and understanding of Whitechapel.

5) Having a good knowledge of crime and punishment in Whitechapel will also help you to answer both parts of Question 2, which are about analysing sources.

6) You'll need to use your knowledge to put the sources into context — use what you know to help you make judgements about each source. Don't just bring in random bits of information — make sure you stick to stuff that's relevant to the question.

> The Knowledge and Understanding activities in the Whitechapel section of this book will help you to learn the important facts you'll need for this part of the exam.

Skills for the Historic Environment

You'll also have to Analyse two different Sources

Source Analysis

In Question 2 of the <u>Historic Environment</u> section, you'll be given <u>two sources</u>:

1) Question 2(a) will ask you to consider <u>how useful</u> the sources are for a particular investigation. The <u>investigation</u> will have always a <u>specific focus</u>.

> How useful are Sources A and B for studying levels of poverty in Whitechapel? Use both sources and your own knowledge to support your answer.   [8 marks]

2) For each source, you should think about:
   - The <u>date</u> — when it was produced
   - The <u>author</u> — who produced it and where
   - The <u>purpose</u> — why it might have been produced
   - The <u>content</u> — what the source shows

> You may be given both written and visual sources, but you should handle them both in the same way.

3) In your answer, you'll need to explain how these factors affect the <u>usefulness</u> of the source.

> For example, this image is <u>useful for studying</u> how poor some residents of Whitechapel were because it shows people <u>sleeping in sheds</u> that <u>open out onto the streets</u>, where animals and other people are wandering. This can help us to <u>understand the desperate conditions</u> that some of the population of Whitechapel had to live in.

© Granger Historical Picture Archive / Alamy Stock Photo

4) Question 2(b) in the exam will ask you <u>how</u> you'd use <u>one</u> of the two sources to <u>find out more</u> about the issue in the first part of the question.

5) You'll be asked for <u>four</u> <u>pieces</u> of information — you'll get a mark for <u>each one</u>.

> How could you further investigate Source A to learn more about levels of poverty in Whitechapel?   [4 marks]

1) First, you need to <u>identify</u> a <u>detail</u> in the source that you'd like to <u>investigate</u>. For written sources, a detail could be a short <u>extract</u> from the text. For image sources, it could be something that <u>features in the image</u>.

2) Then you need to create a <u>question</u> that will help you find out <u>a bit more information</u> about the <u>detail</u> that you've picked out. Your <u>question</u> should help you <u>follow up</u> on the <u>issue</u> that's been identified in the first part of the <u>exam question</u>.

3) After you've written your <u>question</u>, you need to say which <u>type of source</u> you could use to <u>answer</u> it. Think about what <u>kind of information</u> you need to answer your question and then identify a source that could <u>tell you</u> that information.

4) Finally, you need to <u>explain how</u> the source will help you to <u>answer</u> the question. It's a good idea to think about the <u>strengths</u> of the source and why it would be <u>useful</u> for your investigation.

> The <u>Source Analysis</u> activities in this book will help you to practise <u>understanding</u> sources, analysing their <u>usefulness</u> and using them to plan your own <u>historical investigations</u>.

EXAM TIP

Barbecue sauce has no weaknesses...

It might seem difficult to know what to look for when you're analysing a source, but the activities in the Historic Environment section of this book will help you get the hang of it.

Anglo-Saxon Crime and Punishment

In Anglo-Saxon England, <u>crime</u> was taken very seriously and <u>punishments</u> could be very <u>harsh</u>.

The King decided what was Considered a Crime

1) In Anglo-Saxon England, <u>kings</u> issued their own <u>law codes</u> stating what counted as a <u>crime</u> under their rule and how <u>severe</u> the <u>punishment</u> should be for each offence.

2) <u>Actions</u> that are considered to be <u>crimes</u> can be split into <u>three</u> general categories:

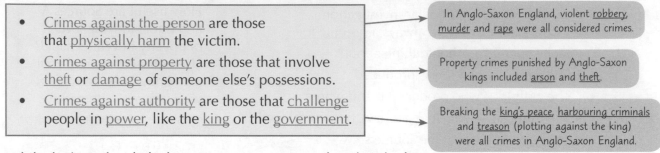

- <u>Crimes against the person</u> are those that <u>physically harm</u> the victim.
- <u>Crimes against property</u> are those that involve <u>theft</u> or <u>damage</u> of someone else's possessions.
- <u>Crimes against authority</u> are those that <u>challenge</u> people in <u>power</u>, like the <u>king</u> or the <u>government</u>.

> In Anglo-Saxon England, violent <u>robbery</u>, <u>murder</u> and <u>rape</u> were all considered crimes.

> Property crimes punished by Anglo-Saxon kings included <u>arson</u> and <u>theft</u>.

> Breaking the <u>king's peace</u>, <u>harbouring criminals</u> and <u>treason</u> (plotting against the king) were all crimes in Anglo-Saxon England.

3) While the <u>king</u> decided what actions were <u>crimes</u>, the <u>Church</u> also enforced its <u>own laws</u> against <u>moral crimes</u> like <u>blasphemy</u> (insulting or mocking the Church).

Punishments focused on Deterrence and Retribution

1) Anglo-Saxon punishments had two key aims — to <u>stop</u> people committing <u>further crimes</u> (deterrence) and to make the criminal <u>pay</u> for their crime (retribution).

2) <u>Corporal punishment</u> (causing <u>physical harm</u> to the body) and <u>capital punishment</u> (death by execution) were both used. The <u>severity</u> of the punishment depended on the <u>type of crime</u> and how <u>serious</u> it was.

- <u>Serious crimes</u>, such as <u>murder</u>, <u>arson</u>, <u>theft</u> or <u>treason</u>, could be punished by <u>death</u> (e.g. hanging or beheading).
- <u>Lesser crimes</u>, such as making <u>false accusations</u> or manufacturing <u>fake coins</u>, could be punished by <u>mutilation</u> — the <u>removal</u> of <u>body parts</u>.
- Crimes committed by <u>slaves</u> were usually punished by <u>flogging</u> (whipping).

> The <u>scars</u> and <u>permanent damage</u> caused by these <u>corporal punishments</u> were meant to be a <u>visible deterrent</u>.

> Anglo-Saxon slaves were <u>peasant workers</u> who were owned by other people. They were considered <u>property</u>.

3) Some punishments were meant to <u>shame</u> the offender to <u>deter</u> them and others from committing crime. For example, for <u>minor offences</u> like <u>drunkenness</u>, an offender might have their <u>legs</u> locked into the <u>stocks</u> or have their <u>head</u> and <u>arms</u> secured in the <u>pillory</u> in a <u>public place</u> — members of the community were allowed to <u>shout abuse</u> and <u>throw things</u> at the offender to <u>humiliate</u> them.

The Wergild was an early form of Compensation

1) For certain crimes, particularly <u>murder</u> or deliberate <u>injury</u>, the <u>accused</u> would have to pay a <u>set fine</u> to the <u>victim</u> or their <u>family</u>. This was called the <u>wergild</u>, meaning 'man price' or 'man payment'.

2) The different <u>amounts of money</u> to be paid were set down in the <u>king's laws</u>. If someone was <u>injured</u>, they were owed an <u>amount</u> based on which <u>body part</u> had been <u>wounded</u>. If they were <u>killed</u>, their <u>family</u> received the <u>wergild</u>.

> The <u>amount</u> of the wergild also depended on someone's <u>social status</u>. For example, those who injured or killed a <u>nobleman</u> had to pay a <u>higher wergild</u> than those who harmed or killed a <u>serf</u> (a peasant who worked for others).

3) This allowed <u>victims</u> to get <u>revenge</u> for the crime against them without causing more <u>bloodshed</u>. Before the wergild, families often got into <u>blood feuds</u> where they <u>killed one another</u> in <u>revenge</u> for crimes committed against their family. These feuds could last for <u>decades</u> — paying <u>wergild</u> was meant to <u>settle</u> disputes, helping to <u>preserve order</u> by <u>preventing</u> lengthy feuds.

Anglo-Saxon Crime and Punishment

Have a go at these activities to test your knowledge of crime and punishment in Anglo-Saxon England.

Knowledge and Understanding

1) Using your own words, write a definition for each of the following:

   a) deterrence   c) corporal punishment

   b) retribution   d) capital punishment

2) Copy and complete the mind map below about crime and punishment in
Anglo-Saxon England. Add as much information as you can under each heading.

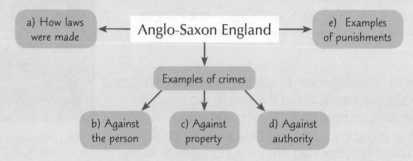

3) Why did mutilation act as a deterrent in Anglo-Saxon England?

4) In your own words, explain how the wergild worked and why it was used.

Thinking Historically

1) Copy and complete the mind map below, by listing evidence for and against
the statement about how crimes were punished in Anglo-Saxon England.

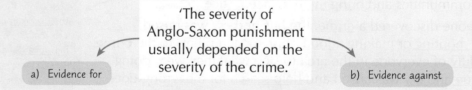

2) Explain whether, overall, you agree or disagree with the statement in the mind map above.

 EXAM TIP

Anglo-Saxon revenge was a dish best served with gold...

*It's important to understand the purpose of Anglo-Saxon punishment. In the exam, you might
get a question asking you how ideas about punishment and its purpose changed over time.*

Anglo-Saxon Law Enforcement

Maintaining <u>law</u> and <u>order</u> in this period was tricky, and the <u>local community</u> had a <u>significant</u> part to play.

The King relied on Others to Enforce his Laws

1) Anglo-Saxon kings were <u>responsible</u> for creating <u>laws</u> (see p.6) and <u>keeping the peace</u> in their kingdom.

2) In the 11th century, England was <u>united</u> under <u>one king</u>, and everyone in the kingdom had to obey the <u>king's laws</u>. However, the king <u>didn't have</u> a <u>police force</u> to investigate crimes and ensure that the law was being <u>observed</u>. Instead, the king relied on <u>representatives</u> to <u>enforce</u> his laws.

<u>Earls</u> were powerful <u>noblemen</u> who were granted <u>land</u> by the king — they were responsible for <u>enforcing the law</u> in the lands they controlled (called <u>earldoms</u>). However, their earldoms were <u>vast</u>, so <u>local representatives</u> were used to enforce the law in <u>smaller areas</u> called <u>shires</u> and <u>hundreds</u>.

A 19th-century artist's impression of a shire court in Anglo-Saxon England, showing an accused criminal on trial in front of local men.

© Mary Evans Picture Library

<u>Shire-reeves</u> (or <u>sheriffs</u>) were <u>noblemen</u> who were <u>chosen</u> to govern a <u>shire</u> (an area about the size of a county) on behalf of the king and the earl. They could summon <u>local men</u> to join a '<u>posse comitatus</u>' to help them <u>catch</u> criminals. They also attended the local <u>shire courts</u> to collect <u>fines</u> and ensure that the <u>law</u> was being <u>followed</u>.

<u>Shire-reeves</u> sometimes <u>ran</u> shire courts if the earl was <u>unable</u> to attend. In the Norman period, <u>sheriffs</u> gained <u>control</u> over these courts when the <u>power</u> of the earls <u>declined</u> (see p.14).

<u>Reeves</u> enforced the law in <u>hundreds</u> — <u>small areas</u> within a shire. A reeve's job included <u>running local hundred courts</u> and <u>bringing criminals to justice</u> on behalf of the king. Less serious issues, such as <u>disputes</u> over <u>debts</u> between neighbours, were tried in hundred courts.

Local People had a Key Role in Catching criminals

Most Anglo-Saxons lived in <u>rural villages</u> — these were often <u>small communities</u> where everyone <u>knew</u> each other. Law enforcement in Anglo-Saxon England was based around these local communities.

1) Ordinary people had a <u>duty</u> to <u>catch criminals</u> within their own communities and <u>bring them</u> to face <u>justice</u>.

2) When someone discovered a <u>crime</u>, the <u>hue and cry</u> was raised. This meant <u>shouting</u> or making a <u>loud noise</u> to <u>alert others</u> to the crime. It was the <u>duty</u> of everyone in the area to <u>stop</u> what they were doing when the <u>hue and cry</u> was raised and <u>help search</u> for the wrong-doer.

Relying on the <u>local community</u> to catch criminals was <u>effective</u> because of the <u>close-knit</u> nature of Anglo-Saxon communities — people <u>lived</u>, <u>worked</u> and <u>worshipped</u> together, so they were likely to know <u>who</u> had committed the crime and <u>where</u> they might be found.

3) <u>Communities</u> were also <u>divided</u> into <u>tithings</u> — these were <u>small groups</u> of <u>men</u> over the age of <u>twelve</u> who were responsible for the <u>behaviour</u> of everyone in their tithing.

4) Each tithing was <u>led</u> by a <u>tithing man</u>. The whole group was responsible for bringing to <u>court</u> any <u>member</u> of the tithing who had been accused of a <u>crime</u>.

5) It was in the <u>interests</u> of the members of the tithing to hand over wrong-doers, as the whole tithing could be <u>fined</u> if they <u>failed</u> to bring an <u>accused</u> member of their group to court.

Comment and Analysis

This system of law enforcement relied on the idea of <u>collective responsibility</u>, meaning that it was <u>everyone's job</u> to make sure the law was <u>upheld</u>. This was particularly important because there was <u>no police force</u> to maintain law and order.

Anglo-Saxon Law Enforcement

The activities on this page will help test your understanding of the Anglo-Saxon system of law enforcement.

Knowledge and Understanding

1) Write a definition for each of the following terms:

   a) Hue and cry   b) 'Posse comitatus'   c) Tithing

2) Copy and complete the table below by explaining the role that each of the following people played in enforcing the law in Anglo-Saxon England.

The king	Earls	Shire-reeves	Reeves

3) Many methods of law enforcement in Anglo-Saxon England relied on collective responsibility. Copy and complete the mind map below by adding information about collective responsibility and its role in the Anglo-Saxon law enforcement system.

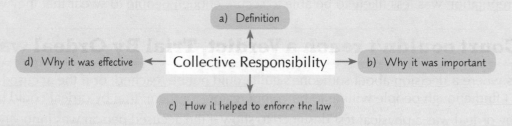

a) Definition

d) Why it was effective   ←   Collective Responsibility   →   b) Why it was important

c) How it helped to enforce the law

Thinking Historically

1) Copy and complete the table below, explaining whether you mostly agree or mostly disagree with each statement.

Statement	Mostly agree or mostly disagree?	Explanation for choice
a) 'The king played an essential role in local Anglo-Saxon law enforcement.'		
b) 'Shire-reeves had little responsibility for law enforcement in local communities.'		
c) 'Tithings played the most important role in Anglo-Saxon law enforcement.'		

EXAM TIP

Catching criminals was hard, but not im-posse-ble...

In the exam, it's important to take a couple of minutes before the start of longer questions to plan your answer. This will make sure that you answer the question and don't veer off topic.

Crime and Punishment in Medieval England, c.1000-c.1500

Trials in Anglo-Saxon England

When someone was <u>accused</u> of a <u>crime</u> in Anglo-Saxon England, they were put on <u>trial</u> to decide their guilt.

Accused Criminals were Tried in Local Courts

1) After a <u>criminal</u> was <u>caught</u>, they would be put on trial at a <u>hundred court</u> in front of a <u>group</u> of respected <u>local men</u> and a <u>local official</u>, normally the <u>reeve</u> (see p.8). This group <u>heard the case</u> and decided the <u>verdict</u> of the trial.

2) <u>Local people</u> played a <u>key role</u> in Anglo-Saxon trials. Both the <u>accused</u> and the <u>accuser</u> produced <u>witnesses</u> who stated whether or not a <u>crime</u> had taken place, but they <u>didn't provide</u> any <u>details</u> or <u>evidence</u> of what happened.

> The <u>tight-knit</u> nature of Anglo-Saxon communities meant that the men in the <u>court</u> were likely to <u>know</u> both the <u>victim</u> and the <u>accused</u>

Compurgation

- If the <u>witnesses agreed</u> that a crime had been committed, the <u>accused person</u> could be given a trial by <u>compurgation</u>.
- In this trial, the accused had to swear an <u>oath of innocence</u>.
- They then had to gather a <u>certain number</u> of local people to act as <u>compurgators</u> — people who were prepared to <u>swear an oath</u> that the accused was telling the <u>truth</u> about their innocence.

> **Comment and Analysis**
>
> <u>Oaths</u> were taken <u>very seriously</u> in Anglo-Saxon England, so the <u>word</u> of <u>trustworthy citizens</u> could be accepted as <u>proof</u> of a person's <u>innocence</u>.

3) <u>Reputation</u> was very important in Anglo-Saxon trials. Whether or not a person was <u>judged</u> to be <u>guilty</u> often depended on their <u>character</u> and whether they were <u>trusted</u> by the community — a person who had a <u>poor reputation</u> was <u>less likely</u> to be able to secure <u>enough people</u> to swear that they were <u>innocent</u>.

If the Court couldn't reach a Verdict, Trial By Ordeal was used

1) In cases where a <u>decision</u> about someone's guilt <u>could not</u> be <u>reached</u>, or if the <u>accused</u> person <u>couldn't find</u> enough people willing to be <u>compurgators</u> for them, <u>trial by ordeal</u> could be used.

2) A <u>trial by ordeal</u> was a physical test designed to <u>show</u> if the accused person was <u>innocent</u> or <u>guilty</u>.

3) This type of test was based on the belief that <u>God</u> was <u>all-knowing</u>, so he could <u>see</u> a person's <u>guilt</u> or <u>innocence</u> and <u>reveal</u> it through the <u>outcome</u> of the <u>ordeal</u>.

4) Most <u>ordeals</u> (except trial by cold water) took place in a <u>church</u>. The accused was made to undergo <u>three days</u> of <u>fasting</u> and <u>prayer</u> before the trial, so they would be <u>pure</u> and <u>ready</u> for God's <u>judgement</u>.

> **Comment and Analysis**
>
> The Church was a <u>powerful</u> institution in Anglo-Saxon England. As well as creating their <u>own laws</u>, (see p.6) the Church played a key role in <u>enforcing</u> the <u>king's laws</u>.

5) The Anglo-Saxons used different kinds of <u>trial by ordeal</u>:

- <u>Trial by boiling water</u> was mainly used for <u>men</u>. The accused had to plunge an <u>arm</u> into <u>boiling water</u>. If the wound was <u>healing well</u> after <u>three days</u>, the accused was <u>innocent</u>, but they were <u>guilty</u> if it <u>wasn't</u>.
- <u>Trial by cold water</u> was also mainly reserved for <u>men</u>. The accused would be <u>tied up</u> and <u>plunged</u> into a <u>deep pool</u> of cold water that had been <u>blessed</u> by a priest. If they <u>floated</u>, the water — and therefore <u>God</u> — was '<u>rejecting</u>' them, meaning they were <u>guilty</u>. If they <u>sank</u>, the water had '<u>accepted</u>' them, so they were <u>innocent</u>.
- <u>Trial by hot iron</u> was mainly used to test <u>women</u>. In this trial, the accused had to <u>walk</u> a short distance <u>holding</u> a <u>red-hot iron bar</u>. As in trial by boiling water, if their wound <u>wasn't</u> <u>healing</u> well after <u>three days</u>, they were judged to be <u>guilty</u>.

An artist's impression published in the 1920s showing a trial by cold water. A priest is overseeing the ordeal from the bridge.

© Mary Evans Picture Library

6) Historians have different ideas about <u>why</u> ordeals were used. Some argue that using <u>God's judgement</u> to decide a person's guilt encouraged communities to <u>accept</u> the verdict. Others suggest that the harsh nature of ordeals <u>frightened people</u> into <u>confessing</u>, or <u>deterred</u> people from committing crime.

Trials in Anglo-Saxon England

Both the local community and the Church were involved in trials in Anglo-Saxon England — have a go at these activities to make sure you understand the role they played, and what each type of trial involved.

Knowledge and Understanding

1) Explain why each of the following were important in Anglo-Saxon trials:

a) Oaths

b) Reputation

2) Give two examples of situations where a trial by ordeal might have been used.

3) Copy and complete the table below by adding as much detail as you can about each type of trial by ordeal.

Ordeal	Who it was used for	What it involved	How the verdict was decided
a) Boiling water			
b) Cold water			
c) Hot iron			

Thinking Historically

1) Write down a piece of evidence for and against each statement in the boxes below.

a) 'Churchmen played a big role in determining guilt in Anglo-Saxon England.'

b) 'Trials in the Anglo-Saxon period were unlikely to accurately determine whether someone was guilty.'

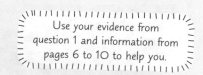

Use your evidence from question 1 and information from pages 6 to 10 to help you.

2) Do you think the Church or local people played a more important role in Anglo-Saxon law enforcement? Explain your answer.

EXAM TIP

If at first you don't succeed, trial, trial, and trial again...

Some of your marks in the exam are for using specialist terminology. Make sure you use specific terms like 'trial by ordeal' and 'compurgation' (if you can spell it) in your answers.

Norman Crime and Punishment

In 1066, the <u>Normans</u>, led by William the Conqueror, <u>invaded</u> England. This became known as the <u>Norman Conquest</u>. William replaced Anglo-Saxon nobles with Normans, but <u>didn't make</u> many changes to the <u>law</u>.

The Normans Kept most of the Existing English Laws

1) The Normans defeated the Anglo-Saxons at the <u>Battle of Hastings</u> in <u>1066</u> and took control of England. The new king, <u>William I</u>, was now in charge of making <u>English laws</u>.

2) William and the Normans faced <u>opposition</u> from many <u>nobles</u> in England who <u>rebelled</u> against Norman rule. There were several Anglo-Saxon <u>uprisings</u> across the country between 1068 and 1071, including a particularly serious <u>rebellion in the north</u> of England in <u>1069</u>.

3) These rebellions were serious <u>crimes against authority</u> (see p.6). William couldn't afford to <u>lose control</u> of the country, so he reacted to them <u>swiftly</u> and with <u>force</u>.

> William responded to the <u>northern rebellion in 1069</u> by marching to the area and <u>devastating</u> it — the Normans killed hundreds of people, burned crops and homes, and destroyed livestock. This <u>brutal response</u> to the rebellion became known as '<u>the harrying of the north</u>'.

Comment and Analysis

William's response to the 1069 rebellion was <u>deliberately harsh</u> — he wanted to <u>stop</u> any <u>future rebellion</u> in the north by removing the rebels' support and supplies, and he also wanted to <u>deter others</u> from rebelling against his rule.

4) In the years after the 1069 rebellion, William <u>tightened his control</u> over England — he <u>replaced</u> the remaining Anglo-Saxon nobles by <u>taking their land</u> and giving it to Normans. Many of the <u>earls</u> who had <u>enforced the law</u> during Anglo-Saxon times were replaced by nobles who were more willing to <u>support William</u>.

5) Although William replaced many of those responsible for <u>enforcing the law</u>, he <u>kept</u> most of the existing <u>Anglo-Saxon laws</u>. He wanted people to see him as the <u>rightful successor</u> of the Anglo-Saxon king, Edward the Confessor, who had died in 1066, so he <u>kept</u> as much of the Anglo-Saxon state as he could.

The Normans Introduced some New Laws

As well as <u>keeping</u> Anglo-Saxon laws, the Normans created <u>new laws</u> to <u>protect</u> themselves and their <u>rights</u>.

1) William introduced the <u>murdrum fine</u> to <u>protect Normans</u> from <u>violence</u>. If a <u>Norman</u> was murdered and the killer <u>wasn't caught</u>, local Anglo-Saxons had to <u>pay a fine</u>.

2) He also introduced <u>forest law</u> to prevent <u>ordinary people</u> from <u>hunting</u> in certain parts of the realm.

- Under forest law, <u>large areas</u> of England were classed as '<u>royal forest</u>' — this was <u>land</u> that was reserved as a <u>hunting ground</u> for the king and certain nobles.

- Forest law denied <u>ordinary people</u> the right to <u>hunt wildlife</u> or <u>gather food</u> in the new 'forest' areas. Those who <u>defied</u> this law were guilty of the <u>new crime</u> of <u>poaching</u> — <u>hunting</u> on <u>someone else's land</u> without their permission.

- The law was enforced through <u>harsh punishment</u> — <u>poachers</u> could be <u>blinded</u>, have <u>fingers removed</u> so they couldn't draw a bow, or be <u>executed</u>.

> Before forest law, ordinary people were allowed to <u>hunt</u> and <u>forage for food</u> in most parts of England.

In Hampshire, villages were cleared to make room for the New Forest — new hunting grounds for the king.

Reaction to Forest Law

- <u>Forest law</u> was <u>unpopular</u> in England because it <u>changed</u> the way many ordinary people <u>lived</u>. Those who had previously been able to <u>live off the land</u> could now be <u>executed</u> for trying to <u>feed</u> their families.

- Many people believed that <u>poaching</u> shouldn't be a crime — they thought the laws against it were <u>unfair</u>. This <u>attitude</u> meant that poaching was a <u>social crime</u> — an offence that is <u>not</u> thought to be <u>wrong</u> by most people.

Norman Crime and Punishment

While the Norman Conquest led to the creation of new crimes, much of the Anglo-Saxon system remained. These activities will help you to explore the impact of the Conquest on the development of crime in England.

Knowledge and Understanding

1) Why did William I decide to keep most of the Anglo-Saxon laws when he came to power?

2) What was the murdrum fine and why did William I introduce it to England?

3) Copy and complete the mind map below about forest law.

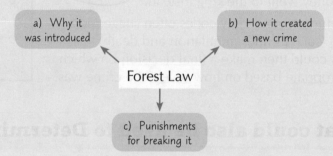

a) Why it was introduced

b) How it created a new crime

Forest Law

c) Punishments for breaking it

4) Explain why poaching was a social crime in Norman England.

Thinking Historically

1) Copy and complete the diagram below, adding information about William's response to the Anglo-Saxon rebellions between 1068 and 1071.

Anglo-Saxon Rebellions

| Response to the 1069 rebellion | Reasons for response | Long-term response to rebellions | Effect of this on crime and punishment |

a)   b)   c)   d)

2) 'William I's laws had a significant impact on Anglo-Saxon communities.'
a) Write a paragraph agreeing with the statement above.
b) Write a paragraph disagreeing with the statement above.
c) Write a conclusion summarising how far you agree with the statement above.

The harshest punishment for poaching? Eggs-ecution...

In the exam, you might be asked about the significance of a factor in the development of crime and punishment. Think about what stayed the same as well as what changed due to that factor.

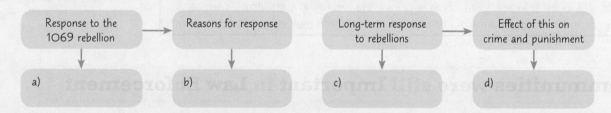

Norman Crime and Punishment

As well as keeping Anglo-Saxon laws, the Normans continued to use capital and corporal punishment. However, the Normans also introduced some of their own methods of law enforcement to England.

Punishments didn't Change much under the Normans

1) The main aims of punishment were still deterrence and retribution.

2) Execution continued to be the punishment for serious crimes such as treason and murder. The Normans normally used hanging.

3) Corporal punishments like whipping and mutilation were still used to punish more minor crimes.

4) The Anglo-Saxon wergild was replaced by a new system of fines. Rather than paying compensation to the victim or their family, the money went to the king instead.

5) By the early 12th century, Norman law codes often suggested a range of punishments (such as fines, mutilation and death) for the same crime — courts could then make a final decision on which punishment was appropriate based on how severe the crime was.

See p.6 for information on Anglo-Saxon punishments and p.8 for more on law enforcement.

Comment and Analysis

The changes to wergild reflect the growing role of the king in law enforcement in the Norman period. The Normans introduced a more centralised system of law enforcement — this meant that matters of law and order were controlled by one authority (the king).

Trial By Combat could also be used to Determine Guilt

1) Trial by ordeal (p.10) continued under the Normans, and they introduced a new ordeal of trial by combat.

2) Like other forms of ordeal, trial by combat was used when methods like swearing oaths and producing witnesses had failed to determine guilt.

3) In trial by combat, the accuser and the accused would fight each other to the death, or until one of the fighters surrendered. The loser, whether they were killed or had given in, was judged to be guilty.

4) Anglo-Saxons could choose to use trial by combat or trial by hot iron to defend themselves if they were accused of crimes like murder and robbery by a Norman.

Trial by combat was also used to settle disputes over land ownership.

A 19th-century artist's impression of what a trial by combat might have been like during the 11th century.

Comment and Analysis

Trial by combat was both a form of trial and punishment, because a verdict of 'guilty' was decided as the loser was killed. Even in cases where one fighter surrendered, doing so would make him guilty, meaning he could be punished with mutilation or death anyway.

Communities were still Important in Law Enforcement

1) People continued to live in small, rural communities, so local people were still responsible for enforcing the law in their area under the supervision of local nobles, sheriffs (shire-reeves) and reeves.

2) The system for catching and trying criminals also remained largely the same. The hue and cry and tithings were still used to catch wrong-doers, and shire and hundred courts (p.8) continued to be used.

There were some changes to local law enforcement:

- The Normans built castles in strategic locations to help prevent unrest and enforce law and order.
- Earls became less powerful, and sheriffs began to act as the king's main representative in the shires, taking over shire courts. Many sheriffs were also given control of castles.
- By 1100, all Anglo-Saxon nobles had been replaced by Normans, giving Normans control over the enforcement of the king's laws.

Norman Crime and Punishment

The following activities will test your knowledge of how law enforcement developed under the Normans.

Knowledge and Understanding

1) Give two examples of punishments that remained the same after the Norman Conquest.

2) Copy and complete the table below, giving details about how the Norman Conquest affected the following Anglo-Saxon punishments.

Feature of law enforcement	How it stayed the same	How it changed
a) Fines		
b) Trial by ordeal		

Thinking Historically

1) Copy and complete the mind map below, giving examples of similarities between local law enforcement in the Anglo-Saxon period and the Norman period.

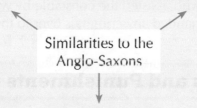

Similarities to the Anglo-Saxons

2) Copy and complete the mind map below, explaining the effect that the Norman Conquest had on local law enforcement in England. Give as much detail as you can.

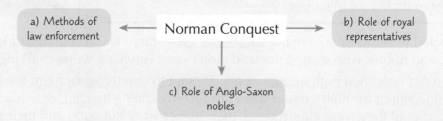

a) Methods of law enforcement

Norman Conquest

b) Role of royal representatives

c) Role of Anglo-Saxon nobles

3) Do you think the Norman Conquest was significant in changing crime and punishment in England? Explain your answer.

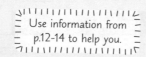

Use information from p.12-14 to help you.

Norman-ly I'd be sorry for such awful puns, but not today...

It's important to understand continuity as well as change — in the exam, you could be asked to explain how a particular aspect of crime and punishment was similar in two different periods.

The Later Middle Ages

In the later Middle Ages, the king gained a bigger role in law enforcement, and more new laws were created.

Law Enforcement became more Centralised

1) In the later Middle Ages, law enforcement was increasingly carried out by royal officials. This created a more centralised system, because the king had greater control over how his laws were enforced.

2) The court system was reorganised in 1166 — royal judges were appointed to travel the country and hear the most serious cases in each area, meaning these cases were treated in the same way across the country.

3) The role of coroner was created in 1194. They investigated suspicious deaths, and they also ensured that any fines owed by criminals reached the king.

> Sheriffs continued to manage local courts and act as the king's representative in each shire.

4) From 1195, the king also appointed officials called Keepers of the Peace in areas where there was disorder — their duty was to uphold the law.

5) In 1327, Keepers of the Peace were appointed in all areas and they later became known as Justices of the Peace. They had the power to imprison criminals, judge cases and hang the guilty.

> **Comment and Analysis**
> By introducing more royal representatives into each region, monarchs were able to ensure that the law was applied more consistently across the country. This reduced the power of communities to police themselves.

There were also some changes in local law enforcement in this period. As towns grew, it was no longer the case that everyone knew each other, so it became harder for communities to police themselves — new roles were created to help enforce the law:

- Parish constables were ordinary men responsible for upholding the law in their area. They did this in their spare time for a year, and weren't usually paid. The constable led the 'hue and cry' and reported crimes to the local courts.

- Watchmen were local citizens who assisted the constable by watching for crimes committed at night. They then handed any criminals over to the constable.

There were New Crimes and Punishments remained Harsh

1) A law called the Statute of Labourers was passed in 1351. It made it a crime to:

> - demand higher wages from your lord.
> - move away from your Lord's land to seek higher wages elsewhere.
> - work for more than a set maximum wage.

> The Black Death (1348-1351) was a deadly outbreak of plague. Historians estimate that it killed around a third of the population of England.

2) This law was created in response to a major social change — there was a shortage of land workers after the Black Death, and nobles who owned the land didn't want surviving workers asking for higher wages.

3) The 1351 Treason Act redefined high treason as any attempt to overthrow or harm the king or his family. A new punishment for high treason was introduced — being hanged, drawn and quartered. The guilty were hanged until they were almost dead, their bodies were cut open and their organs removed, before being chopped into four pieces. The pieces of the traitor would then be displayed in public.

> **Comment and Analysis**
> This punishment was only used around a dozen times before 1500 — many traitors were beheaded or hanged. However, the threat was a powerful deterrent, and it showed that the king took crimes against his authority very seriously.

> The Treason Act was passed to make it clear what counted as treason. Before this, the king's judges decided if an action was treason, meaning there was no clear definition of this crime.

4) From the late 14th century, laws were passed against heresy. Heresy meant speaking out against the Church or its beliefs. The Church felt threatened by heretics (people who commit heresy) during the Middle Ages, so it used its influence to make it illegal.

> From 1382, heretics could be arrested and tried in Church courts. In 1401, a law was passed that meant heretics who refused to give up their beliefs could be burned at the stake.

The Later Middle Ages

Use this page to check you understand how far crime and punishment changed in the later Middle Ages.

Knowledge and Understanding

1) Copy and complete the mind map below, giving details about the roles of the new royal officials in law enforcement introduced in the later Middle Ages.

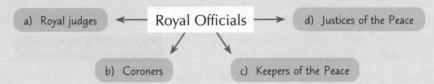

a) Royal judges ← **Royal Officials** → d) Justices of the Peace

b) Coroners   c) Keepers of the Peace

2) Why were new roles like parish constables and watchmen introduced in the later Middle Ages?

3) Explain how each of the following crimes were defined in the later Middle Ages and describe the punishments for each crime:
   a) high treason
   b) heresy

Thinking Historically

1) Explain how the introduction of more royal officials affected law enforcement in the later Middle Ages.

2) Copy and complete the table below by adding examples of continuity and change in crime and punishment during the medieval period. Use information from pages 6-16 to help you.

Area of crime and punishment	Examples of continuity	Examples of change
a) **definitions of crime**		
b) **law enforcement**		
c) **punishment**		

3) Do you think there was more change or more continuity in crime and punishment during the medieval period? Use your table from question 2 to help you.

A Keeper of the Peas looks after the royal vegetable stall...

Don't forget to make sure your spelling, punctuation and grammar are all accurate — there are four marks available for this in the long essay question at the end of the exam.

Case Study: The Influence of the Church

The Church had a significant role in the trial and punishment of criminals in the early 13th century.

The Church had its own Courts for trying Criminals

1) In the early 13th century, the Church ran its own courts to try people for moral crimes.

2) Church courts used some of the punishments that secular (non-religious) courts did, such as fines and humiliation. They could also excommunicate criminals (exclude them from the religious community).

3) However, the Church didn't execute criminals, and their punishments were often more lenient to give offenders a chance to repent (show remorse for their crimes).

> Moral crimes were actions that opposed the social or religious rules of the time. This included blasphemy (insulting or mocking the Church), failing to attend church and crimes relating to marriage, such as having multiple wives.

Comment and Analysis

While the king had more control over law enforcement in this period (see p.16), the Church still had the power to decide what was considered a moral crime and impose its own punishments through its courts.

Benefit of Clergy

- From 1172, any clergyman accused of crimes had the right to be tried in a Church court. This was known as Benefit of Clergy because Church courts would not order the death penalty.

- To claim Benefit of Clergy, criminals had to prove they were a clergyman by reading out a certain passage from the Bible. This was based on the belief that only priests or monks were able to read.

> This passage was known as the 'neck verse', because it could save people from the hangman's noose — some criminals learned this passage so they could escape execution. Benefit of Clergy was extended in the 1300s to all those who could read.

Sanctuary allowed criminals to claim the Church's Protection

1) Since the Anglo-Saxon period, criminals had been able to seek sanctuary in churches — the authorities didn't have the right to arrest them whilst they stood on the holy ground of the Church, which meant they were temporarily safe from law.

2) Usually a fugitive needed to enter a church or ring a certain bell or knocker to claim sanctuary. Some churches had areas marked by sanctuary posts which clearly showed the area within which sanctuary could be granted.

3) There were some limitations to the privilege of sanctuary:

   - In some cases, a criminal had to meet certain conditions to gain sanctuary, such as paying a fine or giving up their property.

   - Sanctuary was also only supposed to last 40 days. After this time, criminals had to either attend court, or they had to leave England.

A 20th-century artist's impression of a fugitive claiming sanctuary.

© Illustrated London News Ltd/Mary Evans

4) However, some churches had greater powers of sanctuary than others — Westminster Abbey had the authority to grant virtually permanent sanctuary, and could accommodate hundreds of people at once.

The Church Stopped taking part in Trials By Ordeal

1) In 1215, the Pope decided that clergymen would no longer be allowed to take part in 'judicial tests'. As head of the Catholic Church, the Pope was in charge of all English clergymen, so his decision prevented them from taking part in trials by ordeal (see p.10).

2) As clergymen were no longer allowed to be involved, trial by ordeal became much less common as a way to determine guilt.

3) However, trial by combat — which didn't require the involvement of a clergyman — continued to be used.

Comment and Analysis

The Pope's decision didn't make trial by ordeal illegal, but it did mean that trial by ordeal couldn't be properly carried out anymore. This shows the power that the Church had over how both secular (non-religious) and Church laws were tried and enforced.

Case Study: The Influence of the Church

The Church was an important institution in medieval England. Use the activities on this page to test your knowledge of the Church's role in defining crime and enforcing the law in the medieval period.

Knowledge and Understanding

1) What is meant by the term 'moral crime'?

2) How were Church courts different to secular (non-religious) courts?

3) In your own words, describe Benefit of Clergy and explain how criminals could take advantage of it.

4) Copy and complete the mind map below to explain the religious privilege of sanctuary.

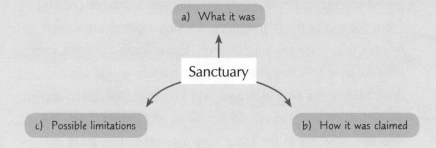

Thinking Historically

1) Copy and complete the mind map below, giving examples of how the Church influenced crime and punishment in the medieval period. Use information from pages 16 and 18 to help you.

2) Do you think that the king or the Church had the biggest influence on crime and punishment in the later Middle Ages? Explain your answer.

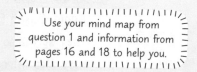

Use your mind map from question 1 and information from pages 16 and 18 to help you.

 EXAM TIP ***You'd be Westminster Crabby if you didn't get sanctuary...***
Don't forget that the 13th century is referring to the 1200s. If you often get your centuries mixed up, try writing out the dates of an exam question in numbers above the words.

Worked Exam-Style Question

The sample answer below should give you some ideas about how to answer question 4 in the exam.

Explain why there were changes in methods of law enforcement in the period c.1150-c.1500.

You could mention:
- the growth of towns
- trial by ordeal

The prompts in the question are only there as a guide. To get a high mark, you'll also need to include ideas of your own that go beyond the prompts.

You should also use your own knowledge.   [12 marks]

It's important to include factors that weren't mentioned as prompts in the question.

Giving specific examples shows you know the topic well.

Make sure your points are relevant to the question.

One reason methods of law enforcement changed in this period was because royal power over law and order was growing. From the end of the 12th century, the king appointed new royal officials to oversee law enforcement. For example, coroners were introduced in 1194 to investigate suspicious deaths and ensure fines owed to the king were paid, and Keepers of the Peace were appointed from 1195 to uphold the law in areas where there was disorder. Keepers of the Peace were appointed in all areas in 1327 and later became known as Justices of the Peace. Justices of the Peace had the power to imprison criminals, judge cases and order executions. The introduction of these officials resulted in an increase in royal control over law enforcement, which made the system of law enforcement more centralised and reduced the power of local communities to police themselves.

In addition to this, the growth of towns led to changes in methods of law enforcement. The growing population in towns meant that it was no longer the case that everyone knew each other, so it was harder for communities to effectively police themselves. As a result, new roles were created to help enforce the law in towns. Constables were introduced to take on some of the responsibilities that had been carried out by tithings in Anglo-Saxon England, such as bringing criminals to local courts. They were also responsible for leading the hue and cry. Watchmen were also introduced to watch for crimes at night. Therefore, the growth of towns led to a more organised system of law enforcement being developed in urban areas, with more specialised roles being created to aid the capture of criminals.

The first sentence in each paragraph links back to the question.

This links back to the question by explaining how this factor led to changes in methods of law enforcement.

This is a shortened example — in the exam, you'll need to write at least one more paragraph.

Exam-Style Questions

Have a go at these exam-style questions to put everything you've learned in this section into practice.

Exam-Style Questions

1) Explain one similarity between punishments that were used in the Anglo-Saxon period and in the later Middle Ages (c.1250-c.1500).   [4 marks]

2) Explain why new crimes were created in England in the medieval period (c.1000-c.1500).

   You could mention:
   - the Norman Conquest
   - heresy

   You should also use your own knowledge.   [12 marks]

3) 'The king played the most important role in enforcing the law in the period c.1000-c.1500.'

   Explain how far you agree with this statement.

   You could mention:
   - Church courts
   - Justices of the Peace

   For the 16-mark question in the exam, 4 extra marks will be available for spelling, punctuation, grammar and using specialist terminology.

   You should also use your own knowledge.   [16 marks]

Religious Changes

In the 16th century, religious developments in England led to changes in the definitions of certain crimes.

Treason and Heresy became closely Linked in the 16th Century

1) Treason (betraying or plotting to betray the ruling monarch) and heresy (speaking out against the Church or its beliefs) were still punishable by death at the start of the 16th century (see p.16).

2) In the 16th century, England experienced a period of religious turmoil — during this time, Catholic and Protestant monarchs changed what counted as heresy and treason several times.

3) In 1534, Henry VIII defied the Pope (the leader of the Catholic Church) and passed the Act of Supremacy, making himself the head of the English Church. This meant that the monarch now had overall religious authority in England, instead of the Pope.

> This change was part of the English Reformation, where the English Church broke away from the Catholic Church. It was part of a wider movement towards Protestantism in Europe in the 16th century.

4) Some Catholics stayed loyal to the Pope and refused to accept Henry as the leader of the Church. Henry punished them for treason because they were opposing the authority of the king.

5) However, Protestants (often preachers or people who wanted England to become more Protestant) continued to be punished for heresy in Henry's reign because he still held Catholic beliefs.

Comment and Analysis

Once Henry VIII became head of the Church, the lines between heresy and treason became blurred — anyone who refused to accept Henry's new status was committing treason as well as opposing the Church of England.

Religious Laws changed according to Who was on the Throne

1) Henry's son, Edward VI, was raised a Protestant. During his reign, England moved away from Catholicism.

- The Book of Common Prayer was introduced in 1549. This was a book of Protestant church services that was written in English.

> Catholics who didn't accept these changes were committing heresy.

- The Act of Uniformity was passed in 1549. This law made it compulsory for people to use the Book of Common Prayer for worship. People who broke this law could be fined or imprisoned.

- However, punishment of heresy was quite moderate in Edward's reign. New heresy laws introduced in Henry's reign were repealed, and only two people were executed for heresy under Edward.

2) Edward's sister Mary I was a Catholic, who wanted to return England to Catholicism. She overturned Henry's Act of Supremacy and created more heresy laws. She also banned Edward's prayer book.

3) Mary executed hundreds of Protestants for heresy — many ordinary people as well as Protestant clergymen were burned at the stake for continuing to practise Protestantism.

Elizabeth found a 'Middle Way' by Compromising

By the time Elizabeth I became queen in 1558, the country had been divided by its religious differences. She tried to create a Protestant Church that would satisfy people on both sides of the divide.

1) In 1559, Elizabeth passed a new Act of Supremacy making her Supreme Governor of the Church of England. She also passed another Act of Uniformity in the same year, making Protestantism the official faith of England, and introducing fines for refusing to attend Protestant church services.

> People who refused to go to these services were called recusants.

2) As a compromise, some Catholic elements were included in Church of England services.

3) However, Elizabeth's approach changed in the 1570s due to fear of Catholic plots against her.

4) While Elizabeth was tolerant of Catholics at first, and few Catholics were executed for heresy during her reign, around 250 Catholics were still sentenced to death for treason.

> In 1570, Elizabeth was excommunicated by the Pope, who encouraged Catholics to remove her from the throne. Many Catholics wanted to replace Elizabeth with her Catholic cousin, Mary, Queen of Scots, who also had a claim to the throne and was a serious threat to Elizabeth. As a result, a Treasons Act was passed in 1571 which made it treason to say that Elizabeth was not the rightful queen.

Religious Changes

Complete the activities below to test your understanding of the changes to the crimes of heresy and treason.

Knowledge and Understanding

1) Why did Henry VIII continue to punish Protestants for heresy after passing the 1534 Act of Supremacy?

2) What is meant by the term 'English Reformation'?

3) Explain the impact of each of the following events on religious worship in England:
   a) The passing of the 1549 Act of Uniformity
   b) Mary I becoming queen
   c) The passing of the 1559 Act of Uniformity

4) Explain why Elizabeth I's attitude towards Catholics changed during her reign.

Thinking Historically

1) Explain the impact of the 1534 Act of Supremacy on definitions of crime in early modern England. Include the following key words and phrases in your answer.

   heresy   treason   English Church   authority

2) Copy and complete the table below, explaining how the definition of heresy changed and how severely heresy was punished under each monarch.

Monarch	Definition of heresy	How severely heresy was punished
a) Edward VI		
b) Mary I		
c) Elizabeth I		

3) Using your answers to questions 1 and 2 to help you, explain why the definition of heresy changed several times in early modern England.

Following the wrong branch of Christianity was tree-son...

It really helps to add some important facts in your answers — a useful date, for example. But make sure they're relevant — the details should be used to support your argument.

Social and Economic Developments

Social and economic changes in the 16th century led to the development of new crimes like vagabondage.

Social and Economic Changes led to an Increase in Poverty

1) The population of England grew rapidly during the 16th century. Historians estimate that around 2 million people lived in England in 1485 — by 1603, the population had doubled to around 4 million.

2) The rising population and poor harvests in this period led to food shortages. This caused food prices to grow rapidly between 1500 and 1560.

3) Changes in farming practices led to poverty and unemployment. Many farmers also switched from growing crops to farming sheep, which was more profitable and required fewer workers.

> By 1500, lots of land had been fenced off in a process known as enclosure — where wealthy landowners turned common land and small strips of land previously farmed by peasants into large farms. For centuries, anyone had been allowed to use common land to gather food and graze animals, but enclosure removed this right.

4) In 1536, the Dissolution of the Monasteries began — Henry VIII closed monasteries across England and took their land and money. This removed a source of support for the poor, as monasteries often cared for the poorest people by feeding and sheltering them.

> The closures contributed to an uprising called The Pilgrimage of Grace. Some of these rebels wanted the monasteries to remain open and for the English Church to be put back under the control of the Pope. However, the rebellion failed, and around 200 rebels were executed for treason.

Comment and Analysis

The combination of these factors led to more people living in poverty, forcing some to resort to crimes like poaching and vagabondage to survive.

Vagabondage became a crime

A vagabond was someone without steady employment who moved around looking for work or begging. Vagabonds became a problem in the 1500s when levels of poverty and unemployment rose.

1) In the 16th century, the government introduced a series of laws to deal with England's growing problem of poverty. The laws gave help to those who were unable to support themselves, like the sick or elderly. However, vagabondage was made a crime, and vagabonds were punished harshly under these laws.

> From 1531, beggars who didn't have a licence to beg were punished by whipping and the stocks. The 1547 Vagrancy Act punished idle vagabonds by forcing them to work as slaves for up to two years, but this was repealed in 1549.

> The Vagabonds Act in 1572 stated that vagabonds should have a hole burnt through their ear, and that repeat offenders could be executed. These punishments were in place until 1593.

> The 1597 Act for the Relief of the Poor meant that Overseers of the Poor had to organise relief for those considered deserving of help. However, vagabonds were still punished by whipping.

2) Vagabonds were punished so harshly because they were seen as a threat to society — it was feared that vagabonds would encourage riots and rebellions against the government.

Smuggling and Poaching were a Challenge for Authorities

In early modern England, the social crimes (see p.12) of smuggling and poaching were common.

1) The crime of smuggling involves moving something into or out of a country illegally. From the 13th century, wool exports from England were taxed and sometimes even banned. Many people evaded these laws by smuggling wool out of the country. In the 16th century, high import duties (taxes) were placed on goods imported from abroad, encouraging more smuggling.

2) Smuggling was hard to police — by the late 17th century, small boat patrols and a force of riding officers had been set up in the south to monitor the coastline. However, there weren't enough officers to be effective against the smugglers, who were often prepared to use violence to escape arrest.

3) Poaching (see p.12) also caused issues for authorities. In the 17th century, only wealthy landowners were allowed to hunt on private land, so poaching was common — enclosure meant people couldn't live off the land anymore, and rising levels of poverty caused many to turn to poaching to feed their families.

4) The authorities struggled to enforce poaching laws — many people ignored them completely, and illegal black market trade in poached game (meat) was common in this period.

Social and Economic Developments

Try your hand at these activities about vagabondage, smuggling and poaching in early modern England.

Knowledge and Understanding

1) What is meant by the term 'vagabond'?

2) Copy and complete the timeline below by filling in the developments in punishments for vagabondage that happened between 1531 and 1597. Include as much detail as you can.

3) Copy and complete the table below, giving a definition for each crime and explaining why these crimes were hard to police.

Crime	Definition	Why it was hard to police
a) Smuggling		
b) Poaching		

Thinking Historically

1) Copy and complete the mind map below about the impact of social and economic changes on crime, describing how each factor changed and explaining how each change caused crime.

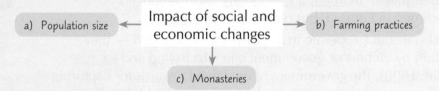

2) Explain how each of the factors below affected definitions of crime in the early modern period.

a) Social and economic changes   b) Social attitudes   c) The government

You can use the information on pages 22 and 24 to help you answer questions 2 and 3.

3) Which of the factors above had the biggest impact on changing definitions of crime in the early modern period. Explain your answer.

Smugglers were always pleased with themselves...

When you're explaining how far you agree with a statement, you can't ignore opinions that don't match your own. You'll lose marks if you don't talk about both sides of the argument.

Early Modern Law Enforcement

Old methods of law enforcement <u>continued</u> in this period, but there were also some important <u>changes</u>.

Local Communities were still expected to Enforce the Law

1) There was still <u>no professional police force</u> in England — local <u>law enforcement officers</u> introduced in the medieval period <u>continued</u> to play an important role in maintaining <u>law and order</u>.

   - <u>Justices of the Peace</u> gained more <u>responsibilities</u> in the <u>16th century</u>, and they continued to <u>imprison criminals</u> and <u>judge cases</u> of <u>petty crime</u>, often without a <u>jury</u>. However, by the end of the 16th century, most <u>capital cases</u> (those where the <u>death penalty</u> could be used) were tried by travelling <u>royal judges</u> instead (see p.16).
   - <u>Sheriffs</u> lost some of their <u>powers</u> in this period as the role of Justices of the Peace grew. However, they still played a role in <u>policing local communities</u> and organising <u>local trials</u>, and they were also responsible for <u>holding criminals</u> in <u>prison</u> until their trial.
   - <u>Constables</u> continued to <u>arrest criminals</u> and <u>bring them to court</u>. They were usually <u>unpaid</u>.

2) Local people continued to play a role in <u>catching</u> criminals — the <u>hue and cry</u> still existed and <u>constables</u> continued to lead it, and <u>sheriffs</u> could still call a 'posse comitatus' to find an escaped criminal (see p.8).

Growing Towns led to Changes in Law Enforcement

The <u>population</u> of England's towns and cities <u>increased</u> significantly between 1500 and 1700. Many people <u>moved</u> from <u>rural areas</u> to <u>towns</u> to search for <u>work</u> — those who <u>couldn't find work</u> sometimes resorted to <u>crime</u> to <u>survive</u>. Towns were also home to <u>successful businesses</u> and <u>rich citizens</u> which created more <u>opportunities</u> for crimes like <u>theft</u> and <u>fraud</u>. This created <u>challenges</u> for local law enforcement officers.

1) <u>Town constables</u> were still used to <u>maintain the peace</u> and <u>arrest criminals</u>, and <u>night watchmen</u> continued to <u>patrol the streets</u> at night (see p.16).

2) However, they became less <u>effective</u> at <u>catching criminals</u> — it was <u>harder</u> to <u>identify</u> criminals among the population of a large town, because it was easier for them to go <u>unnoticed</u>, and people didn't always <u>know</u> each other.

3) Every male householder was <u>required</u> to take a turn as a <u>night watchman</u>, but by the late 17th century, many <u>richer</u> townspeople <u>hired</u> someone else to take their place. In <u>1663</u>, a <u>small salary</u> was introduced for night watchmen in London, but others remained <u>unpaid</u>.

4) <u>Thief-takers</u> also began to operate in the early modern period — they were <u>paid</u> (often by victims or government officials) to <u>find</u> and <u>capture</u> thieves. By the <u>1690s</u>, the government offered <u>fixed rewards</u> for capturing criminals, and more people began to <u>make a living</u> as thief-takers.

© Mary Evans Picture Library

In the 17th century, night watchmen were meant to be armed with a spear-like weapon called a halberd (top right), but many failed to carry them.

Religious Privileges were Reformed in the 16th Century

1) <u>Further restrictions</u> were placed on <u>Benefit of Clergy</u> (see p.18) in the <u>16th century</u>.

From <u>1512</u>, any <u>layman</u> (non-clergyman) who committed certain crimes (e.g. <u>murder</u> and <u>highway robbery</u>), could <u>no longer</u> claim <u>Benefit of Clergy</u>. These <u>offences</u> became 'unclergyable'.	By <u>1536</u>, <u>clergymen</u> were treated the <u>same way</u> as <u>laymen</u> when it came to Benefit of Clergy — they were <u>no longer protected</u> if they committed an 'unclergyable' offence.	During the 16th century, the list of 'unclergyable' offences grew to include other <u>serious crimes</u>, such as <u>rape</u>.

2) The right to seek <u>sanctuary</u> (see p.18) in a church was also <u>removed</u> in <u>1540</u> for more <u>serious crimes</u> like <u>murder</u>, <u>arson</u> and <u>rape</u>. In <u>1623</u>, James I passed a <u>law</u> that <u>officially abolished</u> sanctuary.

Comment and Analysis

These changes reflect the <u>growth</u> of <u>royal power</u> over <u>law enforcement</u> in this period — after the reforms, the <u>English monarch</u> was in <u>control</u> of <u>how</u> the law was <u>enforced</u> against those who committed <u>serious crimes</u>.

Crime and Punishment in Early Modern England, c.1500-c.1700

Early Modern Law Enforcement

There was both change and continuity in law enforcement during the 16th and 17th centuries. Have a go at these activities to make sure you understand what law enforcement was like during this period.

Knowledge and Understanding

1) In your own words, explain what a thief-taker was.

2) Describe how England's towns changed between 1500 and 1700, then explain how these changes contributed to criminal activity in towns.

3) Copy and complete the timeline below about changes to religious privileges in the early modern period. Fill in all the key events, and include as much detail as possible.

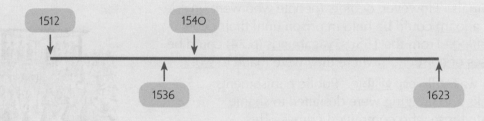

Thinking Historically

1) Explain the similarities between the role of sheriffs in law enforcement in the early modern period and the role of sheriffs in law enforcement in the Middle Ages.

2) Copy and complete the mind map below by giving examples of changes to the role of law enforcement officers between the later Middle Ages and the early modern period. Give as much detail as possible.

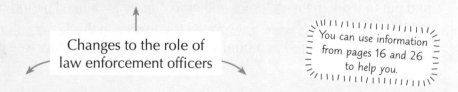

Changes to the role of law enforcement officers

You can use information from pages 16 and 26 to help you.

3) For each of the following groups, explain whether there was more change or more continuity in their role in law enforcement in the early modern period.
   a) the Church
   b) the government
   c) local communities

Religious privileges no longer extended to murder...

You need to be confident about how law enforcement changed over time. The growth of towns in the early modern period meant that earlier methods of law enforcement became less effective.

Transportation and the Bloody Code

In the 1600s, a new form of punishment was introduced, and more crimes began to be punished by death.

Medieval Punishments were Still Used in early modern England

1) In the 16th and 17th centuries, punishments still focused on deterrence and retribution (see. p.6).

> • Flogging, the stocks or fines were used to punish minor offences. For example, whipping was often used to punish begging (see p.24).
>
> • Execution (by hanging or beheading) continued to be used to punish more serious crimes like murder and arson, as well as some cases of theft. Burning was still used for heresy.
>
> • Those who committed high treason could still be hanged, drawn and quartered. Dozens of convicted traitors suffered this punishment in the 16th and 17th centuries.

2) As in the medieval period, prisons were not usually used to punish criminals. However, debtors (people who were unable to pay back a loan) could be held in prison until their debts had been settled. From the 1550s, vagabonds (p.24) could be sent to houses of correction where they were made to work.

3) Punishment was still very visible. Public punishments like the stocks and flogging were designed to shame and humiliate those who committed crimes. This deterred others from committing the same crimes.

4) Executions were also carried out publicly throughout the early modern period, often drawing large crowds of spectators. Executions of London criminals were usually carried out at Tyburn.

© History and Art Collection / Alamy Stock Photo

Around 1571, a new set of gallows known as the Tyburn Tree (above) was built at Tyburn so more criminals could be executed at once.

Transportation was Introduced in the 17th century

1) In 1607, English settlers began to establish colonies in North America. After this, criminals could be transported to these colonies as a punishment — this was known as transportation.

2) Transportation was originally a way of commuting (making less severe) a harsh sentence like execution. Instead of being hanged, criminals could be sent to America and put to work in the colonies, either for life, or for a fixed period of time.

3) While some convicts were transported to America in the 17th century, transportation wasn't commonly used as a punishment until the 18th century (see p.42).

The Bloody Code began in the Late 17th Century

1) From the end of the 17th century, there was an increase in the number of crimes that could be punished by death. This increase in capital crimes is now seen as the beginning of the Bloody Code, the harsh legal system that existed in England from the late 17th century until the early 19th century (see p.42).

2) In 1688, fifty offences were capital crimes. These were mostly serious crimes like murder or rape, or those that threatened the authority of the monarch like treason and heresy.

3) However, under the Bloody Code, hundreds of minor offences against property were made into capital crimes. This development reflected the growing power of England's Parliament.

> In the early 1600s, the monarch was the most powerful authority in England. However, royal power was weakened after the English Civil War in the 1640s, and in 1689 the English Bill of Rights was passed — it limited royal power and gave Parliament more freedom to pass laws. Many in Parliament were landowners who felt the law should protect property — this is why they passed so many laws that punished crimes against property with death.

Transportation and the Bloody Code

Try these activities to check that you understand why transportation and the Bloody Code were introduced.

Knowledge and Understanding

1) Give an example of a medieval corporal punishment that was still used in the early modern period, and explain how it was used.

2) Why were punishments in early modern England often carried out in public?

3) In your own words, explain what the punishment of 'transportation' was.

4) Why did using transportation as a punishment only become possible in the 1600s?

5) What effect did the introduction of the Bloody Code have on the punishment of minor crimes?

Thinking Historically

1) Using the key words and phrases below, explain why the Bloody Code began to develop at the end of the 17th century.

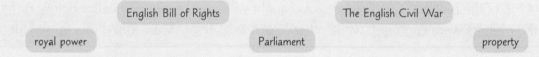

English Bill of Rights   The English Civil War

royal power   Parliament   property

2) Copy and complete the mind map below by listing the similarities and differences between punishment in the medieval period and in the early modern period. Use the information on pages 6, 14, 16 and 28 to help you.

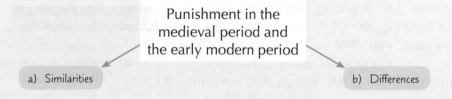

Punishment in the medieval period and the early modern period

a) Similarities   b) Differences

3) Do you think there was more change or more continuity in punishment between the medieval period and the early modern period? Explain your answer.

Transportation didn't mean getting a lift to prison...

When starting a new paragraph in longer answers, begin by referring back to the question. This will help you make sure you've answered the question and all your points are relevant.

Crime and Punishment in Early Modern England, c.1500-c.1700

Case Study: The Gunpowder Plotters

In the 1600s, high treason was seen as a major threat to royal authority, so it was punished extremely harshly.

Catholics were still Persecuted under James I

1) After Elizabeth I was excommunicated in 1570 (see p.22), persecution of Catholics increased. A heavier fine for recusancy (refusing to attend Protestant services) was introduced, and Catholic priests were expelled from England.

2) When James I became king of England in 1603, Catholics were hoping for greater religious tolerance. James was a Protestant, but he was the son of the Catholic monarch Mary, Queen of Scots (see p.22), and his wife was Catholic.

3) At first, James did show a tolerant attitude towards Catholics — he ended fines for recusancy, and he appointed advisors who were known to be sympathetic to Catholics.

4) However, many people still didn't trust Catholics, and James's tolerance was unpopular among some Protestants. As a result, James declared his hatred of Catholicism in 1604 and tightened laws against Catholics. For example, fines for recusancy were reintroduced.

> **Comment and Analysis**
>
> The severity of anti-Catholic laws and how far they were enforced often depended on the political situation in England — Elizabeth strengthened anti-Catholic laws when she felt that her authority was threatened.

The Gunpowder Plot was a Reaction to Catholic persecution

1) In 1604, a group of young Catholic gentlemen led by Robert Catesby began to plot against the King. They wanted to take action against the continuing persecution of their religion.

2) They plotted to kill James I by blowing up barrels of gunpowder beneath Parliament when James was due to be there on 5th November 1605. They aimed to put James's young daughter on the throne, and appoint a regent to rule for her, most likely someone who was sympathetic to Catholics.

3) However, the Catholic Lord Monteagle was warned not to attend Parliament on 5th November. Despite his faith, Monteagle was loyal to the King and revealed the warning to one of the King's advisors. One of the plotters, Guy Fawkes, was caught with gunpowder in a cellar below Parliament.

4) Many of the plotters were captured, while others (such as Catesby) were killed in a gun battle.

Punishment of the Plotters was Harsh and Public

1) Some of the surviving plotters were imprisoned in the Tower of London and interrogated. James gave special permission for Guy Fawkes to be tortured until he confessed.

2) One of the plotters died in prison, but the rest were put on trial for high treason in January 1606 — they were all found guilty and were sentenced to death.

3) The punishment for high treason was to be hanged, drawn and quartered (see p.16). The plotters were all executed in this way, and pieces of their bodies were sent to various areas of London to be publicly displayed.

> **Comment and Analysis**
>
> The brutal punishment of the Gunpowder Plotters sent a clear message that treason wouldn't be tolerated. England was still unstable after the religious changes of the 16th century (p.22), so James needed to establish his authority and deter others from challenging him.

The Plot caused Further Persecution of Catholics

1) After the failure of the plot, more restrictions were placed on Catholics.

Catholics were banned from serving as army officers, voting or practising as lawyers.	Fines for recusancy were increased again.	Catholics also had to swear a new oath of loyalty to the monarch.

2) The plot also sparked an increase in anti-Catholic attitudes in England — many people blamed Catholics for crises like the Great Fire of London and other plots against the life of the monarch in the 17th century.

Case Study: The Gunpowder Plotters

The Gunpowder Plot was fuelled by the religious turmoil that England experienced in the 16th and early 17th centuries. These activities will help you to recap the causes and consequences of this event.

Knowledge and Understanding

1) Copy and complete the flowchart, adding the missing information about the Gunpowder Plot. Give as much detail as possible.

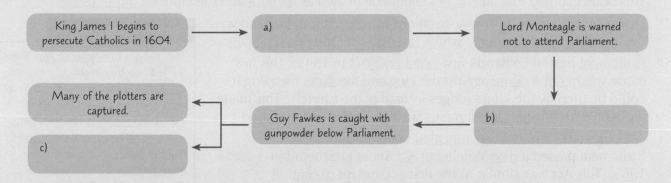

King James I begins to persecute Catholics in 1604. → a) → Lord Monteagle is warned not to attend Parliament.

Many of the plotters are captured. ← Guy Fawkes is caught with gunpowder below Parliament. ← b)

c)

2) How were the Gunpowder Plotters punished? Give as much detail as possible.

3) Why did James I punish the Gunpowder Plotters so brutally? Explain your answer.

Thinking Historically

1) Catholics experienced persecution in England during the early modern period. Explain the role that each of the following factors played in the development of anti-Catholic laws.
   a) the actions of the government
   b) attitudes towards Catholics

2) Copy and complete the mind map below, giving the consequences of the Gunpowder Plot for Catholics in England.

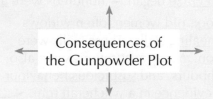

Consequences of the Gunpowder Plot

EXAM TIP

The Gunpowder Plot went up in smoke...

In the exam, you'll be asked to explain how an aspect of crime and punishment was different or similar in two time periods. Make sure you include specific examples in your explanation.

Witchcraft

There was a significant increase in the number of witch trials that took place in 17th-century England.

Attitudes towards Witchcraft Changed over time

In the medieval period, most people believed in witchcraft, and it was generally tolerated as long as people didn't use it to commit a crime. By the 15th century, these attitudes were starting to change.

1) In the late 1400s, a book on witchcraft called 'Malleus Maleficarum' was published in Germany. This book claimed that all witches should be treated as heretics and therefore be put to death.

2) However, before the 1540s, accusations of witchcraft in England were dealt with by Church courts, which did not order the death penalty.

3) Parliament passed England's first Witchcraft Act in 1542. This law made witchcraft a crime against the king and the state, meaning it could be tried by the king's judges instead of the Church. This made it possible for harsher punishments such as execution to be used.

4) Although the 1542 Act was repealed under Edward VI in 1547, Parliament passed a new Witchcraft Act under Elizabeth I in 1563. This Act was similar to the first act, except execution could only be used if witchcraft had caused someone's death.

Comment and Analysis

The changes to witchcraft laws during the 16th century highlight how easily definitions of crimes could change in this period because of the will of individual monarchs. As with heresy and treason (see p.22), the monarch had the power to decide whether witchcraft was a crime, and how it should be punished during their reign.

Witchcraft Laws became more Strict under James I

1) In 1597, James I published a book in Scotland called 'Demonology' which outlined his beliefs on the evils of witchcraft and magic. It was published in England in 1603 when James became king of England.

2) The book explained his views on the trial and punishment of witches — if they were found guilty, James believed they should be executed.

3) In 1604, James I passed a new, stricter Witchcraft Act that reflected his personal intolerance of witchcraft. This law expanded the use of the death penalty to include anyone found guilty of calling up evil spirits or keeping 'familiars'.

'Familiars' were sinister animals that witches could supposedly command. People believed that animals such as cats, dogs or spiders were sent by the Devil to assist witches with their magic.

Comment and Analysis

The widespread use of the printing press helped the ideas in books such as 'Demonology' and 'Malleus Maleficarum' to spread, causing the paranoia over witches to grow rapidly.

Witch Trials became Common in 17th-century England

As the fear of witchcraft grew, a witch craze began — hundreds were accused of witchcraft and put on trial.

1) Many who were accused were poor, old women, often widows or local 'wise women' who had healing skills. These skills were increasingly viewed with suspicion. Many accusations were also a result of grudges between neighbours, and suspicious behaviour from years ago might be used as evidence in a witchcraft trial.

In this period, people began to believe that their misfortune was caused by the actions of witches — when people suffered from an illness or a poor harvest, they often looked for a 'witch' to blame.

2) Those accused of witchcraft were tested to see if they were guilty. The main methods for testing witches at this time included using the 'swimming test' or searching their body for a Devil's mark (see p.34).

The swimming test was similar to a medieval trial by cold water (see p.10). The accused was tied up and lowered into a river or pond. If they floated, the water had 'rejected' them, so they were guilty. If they sank, the water had 'accepted' them, so they were innocent.

3) Religion had a key role in the judgement of guilt in witch trials. Witches were believed to worship the Devil rather than God. It was thought that people who had abandoned God would float in the swimming test, and this was considered enough 'evidence' to convict someone.

Crime and Punishment in Early Modern England, c.1500-c.1700

Witchcraft

Changes in witchcraft laws in the early modern period were due to a wide range of different factors. Use the activities below to improve your understanding of how and why witchcraft laws developed over time.

Knowledge and Understanding

1) How did attitudes towards witchcraft start to change in the medieval period?

2) Witchcraft was dealt with by Church courts before the 1540s.
    Why was this significant for the punishment of witchcraft?

3) Copy and complete the timeline below, describing how witchcraft
    laws and the punishment for witchcraft changed in each year.

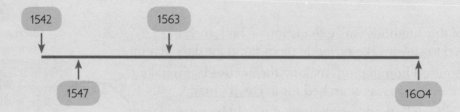

4) In your own words, explain what the witch craze was.

Thinking Historically

1) In your own words, explain the similarities between the swimming test in the 17th century and trial by ordeal in the medieval period. Use the information on pages 10 and 32 to help you.

2) Copy and complete the mind map below, explaining how each factor led to witch trials becoming more common in the 16th century and early 17th century.

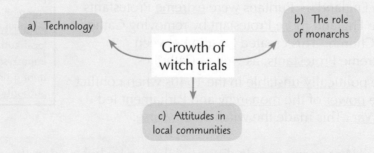

EXAM TIP

Witch trials gave innocent people a sinking feeling...

When considering if one factor is more important than another, it's good to think about how many other things it impacts. The most important factors normally have many consequences.

Case Study: Hopkins and Witch-hunts

Matthew Hopkins became famous in the 1640s for hunting out witches and putting them on trial.

Matthew Hopkins was England's most famous 'Witch finder'

1) Matthew Hopkins was a witch finder — someone with a reputation for being skilled at hunting out witches. Between 1645-1647, Hopkins was involved in the trials of around 250 accused witches across south-eastern England.

2) Hopkins was influenced by James I's 'Demonology'. He capitalised on the growing witch craze by charging towns and villages for his witch finding services. Hopkins turned suspicion and ill will in these villages into cases against the accused, which would then result in a trial.

3) In 1645, Hopkins accused 36 women of witchcraft in the town of Manningtree, Essex. Nineteen of those women were hanged as witches.

4) Hopkins used harsh techniques to persuade those accused to 'confess':

An engraving of Matthew Hopkins from around the early 19th century.

- One of this methods was exhaustion — he forced the accused to stay awake or made them stand for days at a time.
- He also used humiliation, making the accused strip naked while their body was searched for a 'Devil's mark'.
- Once a 'Devil's mark' was found, it would be pricked with pins. If the accused felt no pain, they could be found guilty.

The 'Devil's mark' could be any scar, mole, boil or birthmark from which a familiar could suck the witch's blood.

5) Hopkins created a pamphlet called 'The Discovery of Witches' in 1647 which defined witchcraft and justified his methods.

6) Historians estimate that at least 100 people were executed as witches because of the work of Matthew Hopkins.

Comment and Analysis

Hopkins' pamphlet was partly a response to criticism of his methods — some felt that he was profiting unfairly from the witch craze by forcing innocent people to confess so he could earn his fees.

The Hopkins Witch-hunts were unusually Intense

Hopkins' witch-hunts took place at a time when religious and political changes had made England particularly unstable:

1) Religious division created by the English Reformation (see p.22) was still causing tension. By the 1630s, Puritans had gained lots of political power in England — Puritans were extreme Protestants who wanted to make England more Protestant by removing Catholic influences from the Church. This created tension between Puritans and less extreme Protestants, as well as Catholics.

2) The country became politically unstable in the 1640s when conflict over religion and the power of the monarchy and Parliament led to the English Civil War. This made the witch craze worse:

Comment and Analysis

Some historians have argued that prosecutions of witches were more common during periods of political instability — they suggest that local authorities used witch trials to impose some order on communities during times when they felt their authority was threatened.

- During the Civil War, many people distrusted those who behaved or thought differently to them, which encouraged people to suspect others of witchcraft.
- The Civil War also led to a breakdown in law and order, which caused some communities to take the law into their own hands. This made it easier for dishonest people and witch finders like Hopkins to escalate fear about witches into panic, which they could then take advantage of.

Crime and Punishment in Early Modern England, c.1500-c.1700

Case Study: Hopkins and Witch-hunts

Hopkins was responsible for many witch trials during an unstable time in England. The activities below will help you to understand why the instability in the 1640s made Hopkins' witch trials so intense.

Knowledge and Understanding

1) Who was Matthew Hopkins and how did he help to stir up the witch craze in the 1640s?

2) Why was Hopkins criticised by some people and how did he respond to this criticism?

3) Copy and complete the table below, describing the different techniques used by Hopkins to get people to confess to witchcraft.

Technique	Description
a) **Exhaustion**	
b) **Humiliation**	

4) What is meant by the term 'Puritan'?

5) Explain why there was religious and political instability in England in the 1630s and 1640s. Include the following key words and phrases in your answer.

English Reformation   Puritans   the monarchy   Parliament   English Civil War

Thinking Historically

1) Explain why the religious and political instability in the 1630s and 1640s might have made the witch craze worse. Use your answer to question 5 above to help you.

2) Which of the factors in the boxes below do you think was the most significant in fuelling the witch craze in the 1640s? Explain your answer. Use your mind map on page 33 and the information on pages 32-34 to help you.

Technology   The role of monarchs   Attitudes in local communities   The role of Matthew Hopkins   Political instability

Which finder? A witch-finder...

The witch craze was caused by a combination of factors. If you're asked to explain why it happened, think about how these factors affected the development of witchcraft laws and trials.

Crime and Punishment in Early Modern England, c.1500-c.1700

Worked Exam-Style Question

This sample answer will help you to answer the 4-mark question in the exam. Your answer to this question doesn't need to be long, but you'll need to write enough to get all four marks.

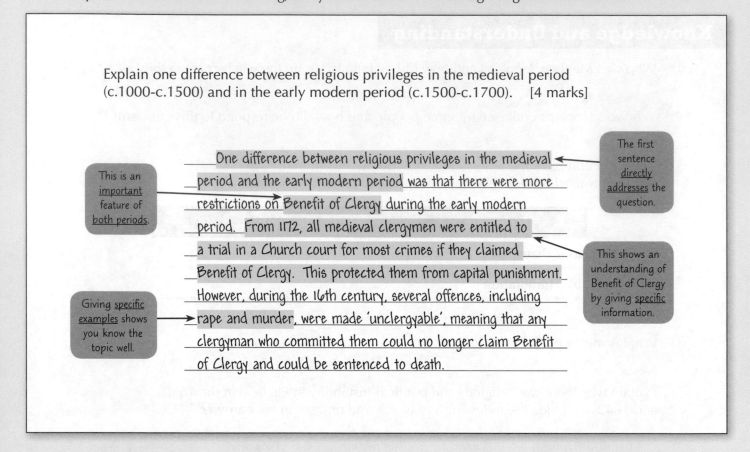

Explain one difference between religious privileges in the medieval period (c.1000-c.1500) and in the early modern period (c.1500-c.1700).   [4 marks]

This is an important feature of both periods.

One difference between religious privileges in the medieval period and the early modern period was that there were more restrictions on Benefit of Clergy during the early modern period. From 1172, all medieval clergymen were entitled to a trial in a Church court for most crimes if they claimed Benefit of Clergy. This protected them from capital punishment. However, during the 16th century, several offences, including rape and murder, were made 'unclergyable', meaning that any clergyman who committed them could no longer claim Benefit of Clergy and could be sentenced to death.

The first sentence directly addresses the question.

This shows an understanding of Benefit of Clergy by giving specific information.

Giving specific examples shows you know the topic well.

Crime and Punishment in Early Modern England, c.1500-c.1700

Exam-Style Questions

Try answering the questions below to make sure you understand everything you've learned about crime and punishment in the early modern period. You'll need to use your knowledge of the medieval period too.

Exam-Style Questions

1) Explain one similarity between law enforcement in towns in the medieval period (c.1000-c.1500) and in the early modern period (c.1500-c.1700). [4 marks]

2) Explain why there were changes in how criminals were punished in the early modern period (c.1500-c.1700).

   You could mention:
   • Benefit of Clergy
   • transportation

   You should also use your own knowledge. [12 marks]

3) 'Changes in society were the main factor in changing definitions of crime in the period c.1000-c.1700.'

   Explain how far you agree with this statement.

   You could mention:
   • vagabondage
   • James I

   For the 16-mark question in the exam, 4 extra marks will be available for spelling, punctuation, grammar and using specialist terminology.

   You should also use your own knowledge. [16 marks]

Poaching, Smuggling and Robbery

In the 18th century and 19th century, poaching, smuggling and highway robbery were all very common.

Poaching was Punished Severely

Poaching first became a crime when Norman 'forest law' was introduced (see p.12). It remained a common crime in the 18th and 19th centuries.

1) Most poachers were individuals who were trying to feed themselves and their families, but others formed organised gangs. These gangs worked together to hunt large numbers of animals, before selling them on.

2) In the 18th century, the government responded to a rise in these gangs by making the punishments for poaching more severe. In 1723, the Waltham Black Act was passed — this Act made it a capital crime to be in a hunting area while carrying hunting equipment and having a blackened face (a disguise commonly used by poachers).

> The Waltham Black Act was part of the Bloody Code (see p.28 and p.42). In total, the Act introduced the death penalty for around fifty minor crimes.

3) The Waltham Black Act was viewed as extremely harsh by ordinary people. The new punishments were seen as excessive compared to the offences, and they affected individuals as well as gangs. The law was also considered unfair, as wealthy landowners were still allowed to hunt wherever they wanted (see p.24).

4) The law was repealed in 1823 as part of Robert Peel's reforms (see p.50), but poaching was still banned.

Smuggling became more Common in the 18th century

1) In the 18th century, smuggling (see p.24) increased in England. Taxes had been placed on more imported goods in the late 1600s, making smuggling more attractive. Trade had also grown — there were lots of items produced overseas such as tea and tobacco that people wanted to buy.

2) Smugglers took advantage of popular demand by forming gangs to conduct larger smuggling operations.

3) The authorities struggled to stop smuggling. It usually happened at night in secluded coastal areas, making it difficult to monitor. The public also often supported smugglers — smuggled goods were cheaper to buy than legally imported goods, and some smugglers were even viewed as heroes.

> One of the most notorious smuggling gangs was the Hawkhurst Gang. They ran a large-scale smuggling operation on the south coast of England in the 1730s and 1740s, and were known for their violent methods.

4) Smuggling decreased from the late 18th century. This was partly because the government reduced taxes on imported goods like tea so that people had less incentive to smuggle. The building of watchtowers on the south coast and the creation of a Coast Guard in the 1820s also made it easier to catch smugglers.

Highway Robbery was a Big Problem in the 18th century

Highway robbers attacked travellers and threatened them into giving up their items. Highway robbers who rode horses were called highwaymen.

1) There were several reasons why highway robbery was such a big problem:

- The banking system wasn't very developed, so people often carried valuables or large sums of money around with them.
- Towns were often spaced far apart, so travellers had to use long roads in remote rural areas, where it was easy for highway robbers to attack.
- People had started to use carriages more — lots of people travelled by stagecoach, an early form of public transport. These were attractive to highway robbers because they could steal from several people at once.

An illustration showing two highwaymen robbing a carriage (from around 1720).

© Mary Evans Picture Library

2) In the 1830s, there was a sudden decrease in highway robbery. This was partly due to the introduction of patrols on major roads to discourage highwaymen. In addition to this, enclosure (see p.24) and turnpike gates (where travellers had to pay a toll to pass) made it harder for highwaymen to escape after a robbery. There was also an increase in the use of banknotes, which could be traced more easily when stolen.

Poaching, Smuggling and Robbery

The authorities struggled to deal with poaching, smuggling and highway robbery. The activities on this page will help you to understand why these crimes were such a problem and what the authorities did about them.

Knowledge and Understanding

1) Copy and complete the mind map below to explain what the Waltham Black Act was.

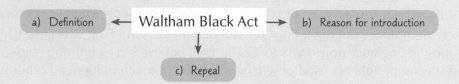

a) Definition ← Waltham Black Act → b) Reason for introduction

c) Repeal

2) Explain who the Hawkhurst Gang were.

3) Copy and complete the diagram below, explaining why smuggling became more of a problem in the 18th century, why it was hard to police, and how the authorities responded to the problem. Try to give as much detail as possible.

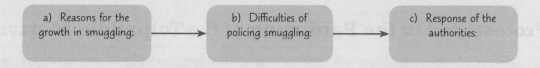

a) Reasons for the growth in smuggling: → b) Difficulties of policing smuggling: → c) Response of the authorities:

Thinking Historically

1) Explain why the Waltham Black Act could be considered a turning point in the punishment of minor crime. Use the information on pages 28 and 38 to help you.

2) Copy and complete the table below about changes in highway robbery. Explain how each factor contributed to the growth of highway robbery in the 18th century. Then, explain how changes to each factor led to a decline in highway robbery in the 1830s.

Factor	Growth	Decline
a) Banking system		
b) Transport system		

EXAM TIP

The problem of poaching was in danger of boiling over...

You might get an exam question on the similarities or differences between certain crimes, such as poaching, in different periods. Make sure you know specific details about each type of crime.

Crime and Punishment in Britain, c.1700-c.1900

Changing Definitions of Crime

In the 17th century and 18th century, some changing attitudes led to changes to the law and its enforcement.

Views on Witchcraft were Changing

1) In the late 17th century, accusations of witchcraft and prosecutions for practising witchcraft declined.

2) Developments in scientific understanding partly explain this change. The Royal Society was set up in 1660 to promote science and academic study. The Society encouraged people to value science over superstitions, which caused a lot of educated people to question whether witchcraft actually existed.

3) As a result, the number of convictions for witchcraft fell. John Holt was Lord Chief Justice (an important legal position in England) from 1689 to 1710. Holt believed in examining evidence closely, and he acquitted several people accused of witchcraft. His approach influenced other judges to do the same.

4) In 1736, the government passed a new Witchcraft Act, which repealed the previous laws about witchcraft. This made it illegal for someone to claim they had magical powers or to pretend to use them — these actions were punishable by a fine or time in prison.

Comment and Analysis

The 1736 Act stated that witchcraft was not real. This shows how changing attitudes among educated people in British society led to a change in the law.

Although the authorities insisted witchcraft wasn't real, many ordinary people continued to believe in it. Some people still used the services of spiritual healers or accused other people of using magic for evil purposes, and locally-organised witch hunts still happened in some places.

Public Protests led to the Pardoning of the Tolpuddle Martyrs

In the early 1800s, the authorities opposed trade unions — these are organisations set up by workers in a particular industry to campaign for better pay and working conditions. In France, the nobility had recently been overthrown by the working classes after a series of revolutions, and the British authorities were worried that a similar thing might happen in Britain if the trade unions were allowed to gain too much power.

1) In 1833, six farm workers from Tolpuddle (a village in Dorset) formed their own trade union. They were angry about wages for farm workers being reduced, leaving them in poverty. They wanted their employers to agree to protect their wages from further cuts.

In 1830, over a thousand farm workers in the south of England destroyed farm machinery in a protest against low pay and poor working conditions. Many were harshly punished for their part in the protest. The Tolpuddle group realised they needed to improve their rights through non-violent means.

2) The six union leaders gathered the support of other farm workers. They asked them to swear an oath of solidarity and pay a subscription to be in the union.

3) The authorities and local landowners wanted to stop the group. However, it wasn't a crime to set up a trade union. Instead, they arrested the union leaders in 1834 and charged them with swearing a secret oath, which was illegal at the time. This enabled the authorities to shut down their organisation.

4) The men were found guilty and sentenced to seven years' transportation to Australia (see p.42). This was the maximum sentence possible, suggesting the authorities wanted to deter others from forming unions.

The union leaders came to be known as the Tolpuddle Martyrs. Their treatment led to public outcry. There were large-scale protests against the convictions — 200,000 people signed a petition against the men's sentencing, and there was a demonstration on the 21st April 1834, where up to 100,000 people gathered in Copenhagen Fields near King's Cross in London. After two years, in 1836, the Martyrs were pardoned by the government and allowed to return home.

Comment and Analysis

The public support for the Tolpuddle Martyrs shows how attitudes to workers' rights had changed — people believed workers should be treated fairly by their employers, and thought this should be reflected in the law. The government's response to this change shows the impact that public opinion had on the way law was enforced.

An 1834 illustration of the Copenhagen Fields demonstration, showing a large crowd that had gathered in support of the Tolpuddle Martyrs.

Petition by Trade Unionists to the King in Copenhagen Fields, 21st April 1834, engraved by W.Summers, 1836 / London Metropolitan Archives, City of London / Bridgeman Images

Changing Definitions of Crime

These activities will help you to understand the importance of changing attitudes for definitions of crime.

Knowledge and Understanding

1) Copy and complete the flowchart below by adding all of the missing events in the case of the Tolpuddle Martyrs.

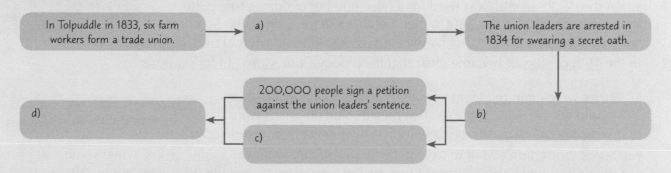

In Tolpuddle in 1833, six farm workers form a trade union.

a)

The union leaders are arrested in 1834 for swearing a secret oath.

200,000 people sign a petition against the union leaders' sentence.

d)

b)

c)

2) Why do you think the authorities responded to the Tolpuddle Martyrs' actions in the way they did?

Thinking Historically

1) Explain how attitudes towards witchcraft changed between the early modern period and the mid-18th century. Use the information on pages 32, 34 and 40 to help you.

2) Look at the factors in the boxes below. Which one do you think was the most important cause of the change in witchcraft laws during the period c.1700-c.1900? Explain your answer.

Changing social attitudes   The role of the government   The role of the Royal Society

3) Copy and complete the table below, explaining the similarities and differences between the government's response to the Tolpuddle Martyrs and William I's response to the Anglo-Saxon rebellion of 1069 (see page 12).

Similarities	Differences

Changing Views on Punishment

Attitudes to crime and punishment were starting to change in the 18th and 19th centuries. The justice system was increasingly seen as ineffective and many people wanted to find alternatives to harsh punishments.

The Bloody Code was eventually Abolished

1) The Bloody Code refers to the British legal system in the 17th-19th centuries when the death penalty was used for a huge number of crimes (see p.28). It began to develop in the 1600s, then became stricter — in 1688, 50 crimes were punishable by death, but by the early 1800s, this had risen to over 200.

> Parliament passed more laws to protect property, which meant that people could receive the death penalty for minor crimes such as stealing goods from a shipwreck or destroying linen.

2) In the 19th century, it became clear that the Bloody Code wasn't fit for purpose:

- Juries were often reluctant to convict someone if it meant they would get the death penalty. This meant some criminals were going unpunished, and crime was actually being encouraged.

> Execution was meant to deter other criminals, but it was clear this wasn't happening.

- Some juries didn't want to treat petty thieves in the same way as murderers, while some religious people also claimed it was against God's law to execute people for minor crimes.

- Prisons (see p.44) and transportation were seen as alternative punishments for less serious crimes.

3) The use of execution for crimes against property gradually declined over the following decades, and in 1861 it was abolished as a sentence for all but the most serious crimes, such as murder and treason.

Transportation was seen as an Alternative to the Death Penalty

1) After 1718, transportation to America (see p.28) became more common after a law was passed making it an official alternative to the death penalty. However, the American War of Independence against British rule began in 1775, and no convicts were sent to America after 1776.

2) Despite this, the government continued to use transportation as a punishment — convicts were sent to Australia (a new British colony) from 1787. As in America, transportation to Australia was used to provide a population of settlers. Convicts were forced to work (e.g. on farms) to establish the colony.

3) If a convict behaved well, they would often get their sentence reduced. Some convicts returned home after they had finished their sentence. However, many former convicts stayed in Australia — some weren't allowed to leave the colony, and others couldn't afford the journey back to England. Some chose to stay because they felt they had more opportunities in Australia.

> Some people in Britain felt that transportation was too lenient as a punishment and that it helped rather than punished criminals.

> At first, most Europeans in Australia were convicts, but later people moved there by choice, hoping for a better life in Australia.

4) Transportation decreased from the 1840s. Australian settlers started to complain about convicts being sent there, and some people in Britain also questioned whether it was effective at deterring criminals. The use of prisons had also grown in England, which reduced the need to send people far away. The last convicts sent to Australia arrived in 1868.

Attitudes towards Public Execution also changed

1) Public executions were meant to deter criminals and show the power of the state. However, in the 1700s and early 1800s, executions were very popular among the public. They were regularly attended by large crowds and often had a celebratory atmosphere — people weren't taking these events seriously.

> The large crowds attending executions caused problems. People often got drunk and caused trouble — some of them might even cheer for the criminal. There were also pickpockets and prostitutes, who saw the large crowds as an opportunity. This meant that more crime was being created.

> In the 1840s, several important individuals, such as the author Charles Dickens, criticised public executions for lacking a serious atmosphere, and for encouraging crime. This helped to shape public opinion on the matter.

2) The last public execution was in 1868 — from then on, executions were carried out behind closed doors.

Changing Views on Punishment

Try these activities to make sure you know how punishments changed in the 18th and 19th centuries.

Knowledge and Understanding

1) Describe what change was made to capital punishment in each of the years below:

a) 1861   b) 1868

2) Copy and complete the mind map below by adding the reasons why there was opposition to public executions in the 19th century. Try to give as much detail as possible.

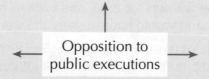
Opposition to public executions

3) Give three reasons why convicts stayed in Australia after serving their sentence.

Thinking Historically

1) Copy and complete the timeline below about the changes to transportation. For each date in the timeline, explain what change happened and whether this led to an increase or a decrease in the number of people being punished with transportation.

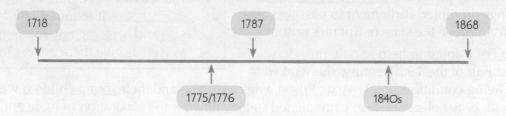
1718   1787   1868

1775/1776   1840s

2) Copy and complete the mind map below by adding the reasons for the decline of the Bloody Code in the 19th century and explaining each one. Try to give as much detail as possible.

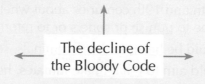
The decline of the Bloody Code

EXAM TIP

A free trip to Australia isn't what I'd call a deterrent...

In the exam, you might be asked to explain why an aspect of crime and punishment developed in a certain way. Make sure you know how changes like the end of transportation came about.

Prison Reform

Prisons were increasingly used during the late 18th and early 19th centuries, but they were usually poorly run and inhumane. The actions of significant individuals helped bring about changes in the prison system.

Prisons Weren't Commonly Used before the late 1700s

1) The use of imprisonment as a punishment was limited in the 1700s. Execution, transportation (see p.42) or corporal (physical) punishments like whipping were more common. Prisons were mostly used to hold people before trial or execution.

2) Prisons in the 18th and early 19th centuries were typically privately owned and often badly run:

   - They were usually dark, dirty and damp. This led to many prisoners becoming ill, often from diseases like dysentery or typhus, which spread quickly in the squalid conditions.
   - Prisoners had to pay prison warders for food, and even to be released. Poorer criminals struggled to pay these fees and would have to share the worst cells with many other inmates.
   - Different types of criminals were locked up together — some people worried that this led to minor criminals committing more crime through the influence of more hardened criminals.

3) Imprisonment became more common as the use of other punishments declined. By the mid-1850s, the use of transportation had largely ended, and the Bloody Code was abolished in 1861 (see p.42).

There were efforts to Improve Conditions in prisons

1) The increase in prisoners and in imprisonment being used as punishment pushed the government to change the prison system. In the late 1700s and the 1800s, new laws were passed that set out improvements to the treatment of prisoners.

2) John Howard, a lawyer, visited prisons around the country to study prisoners' poor living conditions. His findings prompted Parliament to pass two acts in 1774 to improve the state of Britain's prisons.

- The first Act ended the practice of prisoners paying jailer's fees. Before this, prisoners had to pay to get out of prison at the end of their sentence, and anyone who couldn't afford the fee had to remain in prison.

- The second Act aimed to improve prison standards — it required jails to provide a safe and hygienic environment for prisoners as well as give them access to medical care.

3) Elizabeth Fry wanted to help female prisoners. In the first half of the 19th century, she worked to improve living conditions in Newgate Prison, where women and their young children were packed into a few small, dirty cells. She also campaigned successfully for the separation of male and female inmates, the introduction of female jailers, and the introduction of paid jobs for prisoners to earn some money.

There was a lot of Debate about Punishment versus Reform

There were different beliefs in the 18th and 19th centuries about whether the main purpose of prisons should be to punish prisoners or to reform them.

> These beliefs had an influence on how prisons were run (see p.46).

1) Some believed punishments should be harsh to deter criminals, so they felt prisons should be unpleasant.

2) Others thought that prisons should aim to rehabilitate inmates, helping them to become better people and trying to prevent them from committing more crimes in the future.

3) Elizabeth Fry believed in giving prisoners the opportunity to reform themselves and leave crime behind.

> Fry was a Quaker — among other things, Quakers believe God is present in everyone, so Fry believed criminals could change and behave morally.

Comment and Analysis

Many people recognised that the terrible conditions in prisons needed to change, but not everyone agreed with Fry's focus on rehabilitation. Lots of new prisons were built in the 1800s, starting with Pentonville (see p.46), which were designed to be harsh for prisoners. The idea was that the hard experience would deter the prisoners from committing more crimes.

Prison Reform

The prison system had needed reform for a long time, but this only happened in the late 1700s and early 1800s due to many different factors. These activities will test your knowledge of the changes that happened.

Knowledge and Understanding

1) What was the main purpose of prisons until the late 18th century?

2) In your own words, explain what jailer's fees were.

3) Many Quakers such as Elizabeth Fry got involved in the debate about the purpose of prisons. Explain why you think they did this.

Thinking Historically

1) Copy and complete the mind map below to explain why prisons were reformed between the late 1700s and mid-1800s.

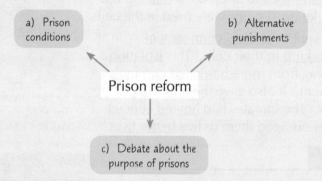

a) Prison conditions

b) Alternative punishments

Prison reform

c) Debate about the purpose of prisons

2) Copy and complete the table below, giving the different ways John Howard and Elizabeth Fry contributed to prison reform. Add as many rows as you need.

John Howard	Elizabeth Fry

3) Do you think John Howard or Elizabeth Fry had the most significant impact on prison reform in the period c.1700-c.1900? Use your table from question 2 to help you.

Elizabeth Fry left the government quaking in its boots...

As well as learning and understanding the key achievements of individuals like Elizabeth Fry and John Howard, you also need to be able to explain why their work was significant.

Case Study: Pentonville Prison

Pentonville Prison was built to deal with some of the problems with prisons in the 19th century (see p.44). The regime in the prison was often harsh, which reflected debates at the time about the purpose of prisons.

Pentonville was a New Type of prison in England

1) Pentonville Prison opened in 1842 in London. Designed by Joshua Jebb, a prison administrator, it was intended to provide better living conditions than many of the existing prisons in Britain.

2) It was built as a result of the Prison Act of 1839, which declared that the 'separate system' should be used in prisons. This system isolated prisoners from each other, which was supposed to allow criminals to be rehabilitated as well as punishing them and deterring future crimes.

3) Pentonville was supposed to be a model of this system and how it should operate.

Pentonville was Designed with the 'Separate System' in mind

1) Pentonville was built with a central hall for the staff that had five wings radiating from it. Each inmate had their own cell positioned along one of the wings — they were designed to provide just enough space for one person to live in.

2) Each cell contained a hammock to sleep on, a toilet and a sink. Heating and ventilation systems were used in the cells.

3) Inmates were typically kept in solitary confinement, eating, sleeping and working in their cells. This isolation was to keep inmates away from more hardened criminals who could influence them. It also gave them time to think about their crimes. The inmates had limited contact with chaplains, who encouraged them to live better lives.

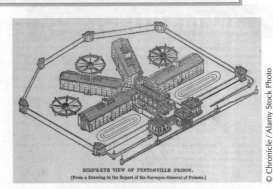

BIRD'S-EYE VIEW OF PENTONVILLE PRISON.
(From a Drawing in the Report of the Surveyor-General of Prisons.)

An 1844 drawing of the layout of Pentonville Prison. The wheel-like structures in the yard were used to isolate prisoners while they exercised in one of the wedges.

Comment and Analysis

The system at Pentonville might sound cruel, but in some ways it was an improvement on the squalid, overcrowded prisons that existed before it — this was a result of efforts in the late 18th and early 19th centuries to try to improve prison conditions.

When they went outside their cells, inmates wore masks to prevent them from seeing each other. During chapel services, they sat in separate booths so they couldn't see anyone apart from the chaplain or speak to each other.

Prisons became Harsher from 1865

1) After Pentonville, 54 other prisons were built using a similar design. However, it soon became clear that the system wasn't working.

2) In the second half of the 1800s, some people believed in a 'criminal class' — lifelong criminals who were thought to be inferior and incapable of change. These attitudes made people think it was pointless for prisons to try to reform their inmates.

3) The Prisons Act of 1865 made life harsher in prisons. Inmates worked for several hours a day, were given dull food and slept on uncomfortable wooden boards. Prisoners were also banned from speaking to each other, which was a feature of another prison regime known as the 'silent system'.

Some people, including the prison reformer Elizabeth Fry (see p.44), argued that the separate system didn't give inmates a real chance to change their ways. Being so isolated also led to more psychological problems and suicides among inmates. However, other people felt that the prison wasn't harsh enough and that was why it failed to deter criminals.

These tasks were often deliberately pointless, e.g. prisoners might turn a handle called a crank for several hours a day for no purpose.

4) The Prisons Act also put all prisons under government control — the government wanted to standardise prisons and make sure they were a proper alternative to transportation to Australia (see p.42).

Case Study: Pentonville Prison

Pentonville Prison was the first of 55 'separate system' prisons to open in 19th-century Britain. Have a go at these activities to make sure you understand how these prisons worked, as well as how people viewed them.

Knowledge and Understanding

1) In your own words, describe the role of Joshua Jebb in prison reform.

2) What effect did the 1839 Prison Act have on British prisons?

3) Copy and complete the table below, ticking the relevant box to show whether each design feature of Pentonville Prison helped to improve living conditions, made it possible to use the 'separate system' effectively, or both. Give an explanation for each choice.

Feature	Living conditions	'Separate system'	Both
a) **Each inmate had their own cell.**			
b) **Cells had heating and ventilation systems.**			
c) **Inmates were kept in solitary confinement.**			

4) What criticisms did people in the 1800s have of the 'separate system'?

Thinking Historically

1) Write down a piece of evidence for and against each statement below about prisons in the period c.1700-c.1900. You can use the information on pages 44 and 46 to help you.

> a) 'The main purpose of Pentonville was to allow prisoners to reform themselves.'

> b) 'The Prisons Act of 1865 was a turning point in the process of prison reform.'

> c) 'The government played the most significant role in prison reform in the period c.1700-c.1900.'

2) Explain whether you agree or disagree with each statement above.

A hammock, a toilet AND a sink? That's what I call luxury...

Remember to use linking words and phrases like 'however', 'because of this', 'as a result' and 'therefore' to clearly show the link between an event and its causes and consequences.

The Development of Police Forces

For centuries, there weren't any professional police forces in Britain — this changed in the mid-18th century.

Urbanisation meant a Better Police System was needed

1) After 1750, Britain's population rose dramatically. In particular, the urban population increased as the Industrial Revolution caused lots of people to move from the countryside to cities.

> The Industrial Revolution refers to the time when large-scale manufacturing using machines in factories became more common.

2) This urbanisation caused further challenges for preventing crime:

- The newly industrial cities were overcrowded, and their large population meant not everyone knew each other. This made it easier for people to commit crime and get away without being recognised.
- Some people became wealthy due to profiting from the Industrial Revolution — this meant they had more money and property for criminals to steal, e.g. from warehouses full of merchandise.
- There was lots of poverty in industrial cities — many orphans and people experiencing poor living conditions committed crimes to earn money and improve their lives.

3) Before the mid-18th century, law and order relied on local people taking responsibility for watching out for and stopping criminals (see p.8). This system was less effective after the Industrial Revolution.

4) Reforms were introduced to make night watchmen more effective (see p.26). However, these men worked part-time and were often unpaid, and they were viewed as ineffective in tackling crime.

5) Thief-takers would catch criminals in return for rewards. However, many of them were thought to be corrupt and involved in crime themselves, and so would increase rather than stop crime.

The Fielding Brothers set up the Bow Street Runners

> Henry and John Fielding were London legal officials. In 1749, they established the Bow Street Runners — a group of men who investigated crime and tried to catch criminals.

1) The first Bow Street Runners were thief-takers who were sent out once a crime had been reported. They also patrolled the streets on foot or horseback.

2) From 1785, the government paid them, but before this they earned money by charging fees for their work. For example, they often charged the victims of criminals they were sent to catch, if those criminals were convicted.

3) The group also published a newsletter called the *Hue and Cry*. The newsletter named and described wanted criminals to make it easier to capture them.

© Chronicle / Alamy Stock Photo

Comment and Analysis

The Bow Street Runners had a big impact on policing — they've been called the first professional police force in Britain. The publication of the *Hue and Cry* demonstrates the key role they had in coordinating and improving national policing.

The Metropolitan Police were a Professional Police Force

1) Although the Bow Street Runners were effective, they were a small group. As London continued to grow, it became clear that a coordinated, government-controlled police force was needed. In 1829, the Home Secretary Robert Peel (see p.50) set up the Metropolitan Police Force to oversee law and order in London.

2) The Metropolitan Police operated in a similar way to night watchmen — they patrolled in organised 'beats' (set routes walked in circuits, see p.76) to deter and catch criminals. However, they were a more centralised and structured organisation than the night watchmen.

> The success of the Metropolitan Police led to other police forces being set up across Britain. The 1856 Police Act made a police force compulsory for all areas — this helped to make policing more consistent across the country.

3) In 1842, the Metropolitan Police set up a detective department to solve crimes. It became the Criminal Investigation Department (CID) in 1878.

The Development of Police Forces

Have a go at these activities on the development of police forces — a turning point in the prevention of crime.

Knowledge and Understanding

1) What is meant by the term 'urbanisation'?

2) Copy and complete the timeline below about the development of the police system in the 18th and 19th centuries. Use information from the previous page to fill in all the key events.

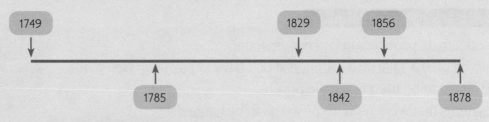

1749   1829   1856

1785   1842   1878

Thinking Historically

1) Copy and complete the diagram below, explaining how each of the developments affected crime in towns in the period c.1700-c.1900.

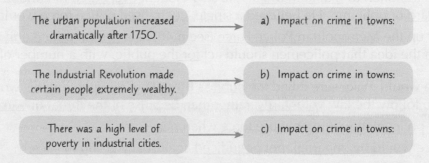

The urban population increased dramatically after 1750. → a) Impact on crime in towns:

The Industrial Revolution made certain people extremely wealthy. → b) Impact on crime in towns:

There was a high level of poverty in industrial cities. → c) Impact on crime in towns:

2) Copy and complete the table below by listing the similarities and differences between thief-takers in the early modern period and the Bow Street Runners. You can use the information on page 26 to help you.

Similarities	Differences

3) Explain the differences between the Metropolitan Police Force and each of the following groups:
   a) Night watchmen
   b) Bow Street Runners

The Neapolitan Police — solving ice cream-related crime...

In the exam, remember to be specific with the information you use. For example, rather than writing about law enforcement officials in general, use specific examples to explain your answer.

Crime and Punishment in Britain, c.1700-c.1900

Case Study: Robert Peel

Robert Peel's ideas about policing formed the basis of British police work and are still followed today.

Robert Peel reformed Criminal Law and Prisons

1) Robert Peel became Home Secretary (the person in government in charge of law and order) in 1822. He believed in preventing crime and allowing criminals to reform, not just deterring them from crime. He made several significant reforms to law enforcement and punishment of crime in Britain.

2) He was influenced by Elizabeth Fry's work to reform prisons (see p.44). He introduced a new Gaols Act in 1823 to ensure the same standards applied to all prisons in Britain.

1823 Gaols Act — Measures Introduced

- Male and female prisoners to be kept separately.
- Jailers to be paid a salary, so prisoners didn't have to pay them (see p.44).
- Female jailers to be used in female prisons.
- Iron restraints that were used on prisoners to be banned.
- Visits by chaplains to be introduced to tend to prisoners' spiritual needs and help them reform.

> A failing of the Act was that the rules weren't always enforced because the prisons weren't inspected properly — regular inspections of prisons didn't start until 1835.

Peel wanted to Change the way the Law was Enforced

1) Peel was concerned that there were too many different police organisations and that the army was being used too often to maintain order. He also thought every area of London should get the same standard of policing. He believed a single, centralised police force would be better.

2) In 1829, he set up the Metropolitan Police Force (see p.48) as a central police unit for London. It was based on the idea that policemen should act for the public, with a number of key principles:

- The force would make sure it had the public's trust. Peel thought that this would encourage people to follow the law voluntarily, rather than because of the threat of harsh punishments.
- The new policemen would only use force when necessary.
- The police would be impartial, not prejudiced against any group in society.
- The main sign that the force was effective would be a lack of crime, as this would mean that people were following the law and society was peaceful.

> British police forces are still expected to follow these principles.

The Metropolitan Police Force Overcame Opposition

1) The Metropolitan Police Force has been considered the first example of a proper, government-controlled police force, and Peel has been called the 'father of modern policing' for his role in its creation.

2) Not everyone agreed with the idea of the new police force, but Peel was able to convince enough people in Parliament to back the legislation he needed.

> Peel also agreed not to include the City of London, an area in the centre of London, in his new force, as they wanted their own police force.

Opposition to the Metropolitan Police Force

- Some worried about risks to freedoms, partly because people in Britain knew about a very strict police force in France that was repressing the French population.
- Some were concerned about the cost or risks to privacy, while some thought policing should be coordinated locally.
- The first officers were poorly-trained and didn't always act morally — this image was exaggerated in the media, which made the new force seem laughable.

3) Some people objected to the new police force because they thought it would be like an army, so Peel wanted to make it clear that the police were not soldiers. As a result, policemen wore blue uniforms, whereas soldiers traditionally wore red. They also carried truncheons rather than guns or swords.

Case Study: Robert Peel

Robert Peel had a big impact on the development of policing, but he also played an important role in prison reform. Try these activities to make sure you understand the changes he made and their importance.

Knowledge and Understanding

1) In 1822, Robert Peel became Home Secretary. What did this make him responsible for?

2) How were Robert Peel's views on the purpose of punishment similar to Elizabeth Fry's views? Use the information on page 44 to help you.

3) Copy and complete the mind map below by stating the principles of the Metropolitan Police Force after it was set up in 1829.

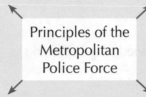

Principles of the Metropolitan Police Force

4) Make a list of the reasons why there was opposition to the development of the police system under Robert Peel. Try to give as much detail as possible.

Thinking Historically

1) Explain how Robert Peel changed prisons in Britain. Include the following key words and date in your explanation.

1823

jailers

chaplains

reform

2) 'Robert Peel had a more significant impact on the development of policing than the Fielding brothers.'
a) Write a paragraph agreeing with the statement above.
b) Write a paragraph disagreeing with the statement above.
c) Write a conclusion summarising how far you agree with the statement above.

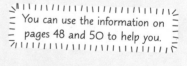

You can use the information on pages 48 and 50 to help you.

EXAM TIP

The Metropolitan Police Force didn't ap-peel to everyone...

Individuals can be an important factor in change, but so can institutions (e.g. the government) and other factors such as social and economic change. Think about all of these in the exam.

Exam-Style Questions

Test your knowledge on crime and punishment in 18th and 19th century Britain by answering these exam-style questions. You'll need to use information that you've learned about previous periods too.

Exam-Style Questions

1) Explain one similarity between poaching in the Norman period and in the period c.1700-c.1800.   [4 marks]

2) Explain why criminal activity changed during the period c.1700-c.1900.

   You could mention:
   - highway robbery
   - smuggling

   You should also use your own knowledge.   [12 marks]

3) 'The government had the biggest influence on how crimes were punished during the period c.1700-c.1900.'

   Explain how far you agree with this statement.

   You could mention:
   - prisons
   - the Tolpuddle Martyrs

   For the 16-mark question in the exam, 4 extra marks will be available for spelling, punctuation, grammar and using specialist terminology.

   You should also use your own knowledge.   [16 marks]

Exam-Style Questions

Exam-Style Questions

4) Explain one difference between the use of transportation as a punishment in the 17th century and in the 18th century. [4 marks]

5) Explain why policing in towns and cities changed during the period c.1700-c.1900.

   You could mention:
   • urbanisation
   • the Metropolitan Police Force

   You should also use your own knowledge. [12 marks]

6) 'Views on the use of capital punishment were completely transformed in the period c.1700-c.1900.'

   Explain how far you agree with this statement.

   You could mention:
   • the Bloody Code
   • public execution

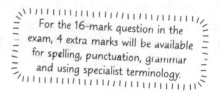
For the 16-mark question in the exam, 4 extra marks will be available for spelling, punctuation, grammar and using specialist terminology.

   You should also use your own knowledge. [16 marks]

Changing Definitions of Crime

Although <u>new crimes</u> have been created since 1900, many of them are <u>old crimes</u> committed in <u>new ways</u>.

Smuggling and Terrorism have taken on New Forms

1) <u>Smuggling</u> (see p.38) still happens today — <u>cigarettes</u>, <u>alcohol</u> and <u>other substances</u> are often smuggled into the country. However, some types of smuggling have become a <u>bigger problem</u> more <u>recently</u>.

> The <u>smuggling of drugs</u> in particular has become more widespread as more substances have become <u>illegal</u> and the demand for illegal drugs has <u>increased</u>. Smugglers who are caught can be <u>fined</u> or <u>jailed</u>.

> <u>People smuggling</u> is the illegal transportation of people across borders. This is different to <u>people trafficking</u>, which involves transporting people against their will, usually for <u>prostitution</u> or <u>forced labour</u>. Both crimes have been a <u>growing problem</u> in more recent years, as <u>organised criminal gangs</u> have become involved in these illegal trades.

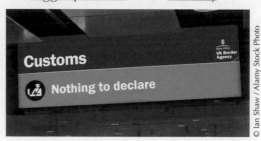

Customs areas in British airports are used to control the substances going into and out of the country.

2) <u>Terrorism</u> was a <u>growing problem</u> in the second half of the 20th century and is still a <u>major concern</u> today:

- The <u>IRA</u> (Irish Republican Army) carried out <u>bomb attacks</u> in Britain during the <u>Troubles</u> (a conflict between the late 1960s and 1998 over whether Northern Ireland should leave the United Kingdom). More recently, bombings have been committed by <u>Islamist extremist groups</u> like the <u>Islamic State</u>.
- In the <u>1970s</u>, the British government began to pass <u>laws</u> to <u>prevent terrorism</u>. After the <u>2005 London terror attacks</u>, which killed 52 people, the government created a law to allow authorities to put <u>restrictions</u> on people who are <u>suspected</u> of being involved in <u>terrorism</u>. Those found guilty of <u>planning</u> an act of terror can also now be <u>imprisoned for life</u>.

> Terrorism is <u>not a new crime</u> — the Gunpowder Plot (see p.30) is an example of a group trying to commit an act of terror in the <u>17th century</u>.

Changes in Technology have led to New Kinds of Theft

1) The invention and widespread ownership of <u>cars</u> have created <u>car-related crime</u>, such as the <u>theft of vehicles</u> and <u>driving offences</u> (see p.56).

2) <u>Computers</u> and the <u>Internet</u> have allowed criminals to commit <u>cyber crime</u>. Criminals now use computers to commit <u>theft</u> and <u>fraud</u> in new ways. Cyber crime also involves illegally <u>targeting</u> or <u>disabling</u> other computers.

> The widespread use of computers has led to <u>copyright theft</u> becoming a common <u>social crime</u> — many people <u>illegally download</u> or <u>copy</u> media such as music, television shows or films <u>without paying</u> for them.

Comment and Analysis

<u>Cyber crime</u> is difficult to <u>prevent</u> because criminals can commit crimes from a <u>distance</u> — often from another <u>country</u>. This makes it hard for police to <u>catch cyber criminals</u>, even if they manage to work out who has committed the crime.

Some Existing Crimes were Decriminalised in the 20th century

1) The <u>1967 Abortion Act</u> decriminalised <u>abortion</u> (made it legal), as long as two doctors agree that certain conditions have been met.

2) <u>Homosexual acts</u> between <u>men</u> were <u>illegal</u> in the UK until the 1960s.

- In <u>1967</u>, a law was passed to <u>decriminalise</u> homosexual acts between men aged 21 or over. However, the law had <u>limitations</u> — men were still <u>not permitted</u> to have sex in 'public' places like hotels.
- More recent laws have been passed <u>decriminalising</u> all homosexual acts and lowering the <u>age of consent</u> to 16.

Comment and Analysis

Governments respond to changing <u>social attitudes</u> by creating new crimes, but also by <u>decriminalising</u> existing crimes. Homosexuality and abortion both became <u>legal</u> because members of the <u>public</u> put <u>pressure</u> on the government to <u>change the law</u>.

Changing Definitions of Crime

Try these activities to test your knowledge of how crimes evolved as a result of changes in modern Britain.

Knowledge and Understanding

1) What is the current punishment for smuggling drugs?

2) Use the information on the previous page to write a definition for each of the following terms:

   a) IRA
   c) people smuggling
   b) cyber crime
   d) decriminalisation

3) Make a list of crimes that involve the use of computers.

4) Explain why cyber crime is difficult to prevent.

5) In your own words, describe the 1967 Abortion Act.

Thinking Historically

1) Copy and complete the diagram below. Describe how each crime changed between the period c.1700-c.1900 and the modern period, then explain the reasons for this change. Include as much detail as possible.

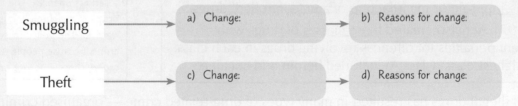

| Smuggling → | a) Change: | → | b) Reasons for change: |
| Theft → | c) Change: | → | d) Reasons for change: |

2) Describe the differences between the government's response to terrorism in the 17th century and its response after 1900. Use pages 30 and 54 to help you.

3) Explain how government action and changing social attitudes led to the decriminalisation of old crimes in the 1960s. Include the following key words in your explanation.

   homosexuality   abortion   public   pressure

People who steal vehicles are punished by in-car-ceration...

Even when you discuss modern crimes, you shouldn't assume that the examiner knows what you're talking about — you still need to back up your points with clear and relevant examples.

Changing Definitions of Crime

Social and technological changes in the 20th century led to new crimes being created.

More Immigration meant Laws against Racism were needed

1) In the late 1940s, after the Second World War, many immigrants arrived in Britain, mainly from the Commonwealth. Many black and Asian immigrants faced hostility from parts of the press and society.

2) This led to racial tension in the late 1940s and 1950s, which caused a series of race riots. In 1958, West Indian immigrants living in Notting Hill in London were attacked because of their ethnicity.

3) The government realised that new laws were needed to protect immigrants from racial discrimination.

> In 1965, the Race Relations Act was passed. It made it a crime to discriminate against somebody because of their race or to promote hatred due to racial differences. However, the Act was limited — it banned discrimination in certain public places, but still allowed landlords and employers to discriminate based on race.

> A new Race Relations Act was introduced in 1968. It became illegal to refuse people housing, employment or public services because of their race.

> Both of these acts were replaced in 1976 by a third Race Relations Act, which made indirect discrimination (disadvantaging a particular ethnic group) illegal, and set up a Commission for Racial Equality to make sure that the new law was being applied.

4) Laws have also been passed to combat other kinds of discrimination — it became illegal to discriminate on the basis of gender in 1975 or disability in 1995. The Equality Act was passed in 2010 to prevent discrimination or harassment based on nine 'protected characteristics', including race, age and sexuality.

Rising Drug Use has led to Changes in the Law

1) In the 1960s, the use of drugs such as amphetamines, LSD and cannabis became more common.

- A series of laws in the 1960s put controls on many common drugs. It became illegal to possess amphetamines or LSD, while tighter measures were introduced to limit the use of drugs that were already illegal, such as cannabis.

- In 1971, the Misuse of Drugs Act was passed. It banned the possession, sale or manufacture of any 'controlled' drugs.

- The 1971 Act also created three classes of drugs with different penalties for offences involving drugs in each class. The highest class (Class A) included heroin and cocaine.

Comment and Analysis

Some drug crimes are considered social crimes by some people — many who use recreational drugs don't believe they are causing harm or committing a serious offence. The idea that taking drugs is a victimless crime makes it hard for the police to combat drug crime, because people are less likely to report those who use or sell drugs.

2) The use of illegal drugs has resulted in many types of drug-related crime — organised criminal gangs smuggle, manufacture and sell drugs on a large scale. Some thefts and robberies are also drug-related — they are sometimes carried out by addicts stealing money to buy drugs.

The Development of Cars led to the creation of Driving Offences

Car ownership in the UK has increased dramatically since the 1950s. This has led to the introduction of new laws that aim to improve road safety.

> It was already illegal to drive when unfit as a result of drugs or alcohol before 1967, but many people were drink-driving anyway. Even after the 1967 Act and a series of government campaigns against drink-driving, it took a long time for social attitudes to catch up with the law. This shows the difficulty of enforcing the law if people don't understand the seriousness of the crime.

1) As cars became capable of greater speeds in the 1960s and 1970s, laws were passed to enforce speed limits on different types of road.

2) The 1967 Road Safety Act made it illegal to drive if the amount of alcohol in your blood exceeded a certain limit. This was intended to stop drink-driving, which had become a serious problem by the 1960s.

3) In 2003, driving while using a mobile phone became a criminal offence.

4) In 2015, the law was changed to combat the problem of driving while under the influence of drugs — limits were introduced for a number of illegal substances and prescription drugs.

Changing Definitions of Crime

Here are some more activities to test what you've learned about changes to crime in modern Britain.

Knowledge and Understanding

1) Copy and complete the timeline below by filling in all of the developments which contributed to the creation of racial discrimination laws. Give as much detail as possible.

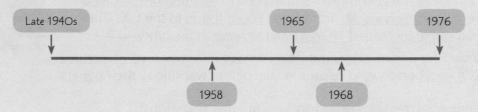

| Late 1940s | 1965 | 1976 |
| 1958 | 1968 |

2) State the developments in anti-discrimination laws that occurred in each of these years:

a) 1975   b) 1995   c) 2010

3) Describe the changes to the law introduced by the Misuse of Drugs Act in 1971.

4) Explain how social attitudes towards drug use make it harder for the police to combat drug crime.

Thinking Historically

1) Explain how each of the following developments in technology has led to changes in the definition of crime. Try to include as much detail as possible.

   a) cars
   b) mobile phones

2) Which of the following factors do you think has been the most significant in changing definitions of crime in modern Britain? Explain your answer.

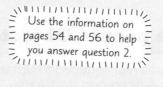
Use the information on pages 54 and 56 to help you answer question 2.

advances in technology   the role of the government   the role of social attitudes

My only driving offence is my novelty number plate...

In the exam, you only have a limited amount of time to answer each question. If you're spending too long on one question, finish your point then move on to the next question.

Case Study: Conscientious Objectors

During the First World War and Second World War, the law was changed in Britain so that people could be forced to join the army. However, some refused to fight — they were known as conscientious objectors.

Conscription made it Compulsory to fight in the First World War

1) The First World War lasted from 1914 to 1918. Millions of men volunteered to join the army, but the government still needed to recruit more soldiers. In 1916, the Military Service Act introduced conscription to the UK. This meant that all single men aged 18 to 41 had to serve in the army.

> There were a few exceptions to the new law — a man didn't have to join up if he was ill or his current job was important to the war effort.

2) The Act allowed for a man to avoid military service if he was a conscientious objector (CO) — a person who refuses to take part in war due to their beliefs.

People became conscientious objectors for a number of reasons:
- Some didn't believe that the war should be fought because they had political objections to it.
- Some didn't believe in taking the life of another human being.
- Some felt that fighting was against their religious or moral beliefs.

> Many conscientious objectors were Christians (and in particular Quakers) who believed that fighting in the war went against their religious principles.

3) Those who wished to be exempted from military service had to face a tribunal (a type of court) to argue their case. These tribunals could be very hostile towards the men.

The Treatment of Conscientious Objectors could be harsh

Around 20,000 conscientious objectors refused to fight after conscription was introduced in 1916. Those who failed to convince a tribunal to exempt them from military service faced an uncertain future.

1) Men who refused to be conscripted could be sent to prison. Prison conditions were very harsh — this sent a message to others that trying to avoid service was unacceptable. Many prisoners were forced to carry out hard labour, while over 70 conscientious objectors died in prison during the First World War.

2) Many conscientious objectors were put to work on farms or in factories.

3) The British Army set up the Non-Combatant Corps (NCC) for COs who were willing to participate in non-violent, war-related activities (e.g. building roads). Men who joined the NCC were criticised by other soldiers and the public for refusing to fight, but also by other COs for supporting the war effort.

Comment and Analysis

The harsh treatment of conscientious objectors didn't stop when the war ended. COs were refused the right to vote until 1926, while many prisoners weren't released until several months after the end of the war.

> Public attitudes towards conscientious objectors were often very negative. Many COs were accused of cowardice — they were labelled as 'conchies' and some were handed a white feather in the street as a sign of their cowardice. The media contributed to this idea by labelling COs as cowards or traitors.

Many more people Objected to Fighting in the Second World War

1) Conscription was reintroduced to Britain in 1939 when the Second World War broke out. Around 60,000 British men and 1,000 women refused to fight.

2) The government showed a more tolerant and respectful attitude towards conscientious objectors than in the First World War. A Central Board for Conscientious Objectors was set up in 1939 to better manage what happened to conscientious objectors and ensure that tribunals were fair.

> There were also several groups who publicly supported COs during WWII. These were represented on the Central Board for Conscientious Objectors.

3) Around 30% of COs were refused exemption by a tribunal. Many others were given a conditional exemption — they had to join the army as non-combatants or carry out work that helped the war effort.

4) Although more effort was made to accommodate conscientious objectors than in the First World War, there was still stigma (shame) attached to refusing to fight, and COs could still be sent to prison. Some men were abused in the street and some employers discriminated against COs due to their objections.

Case Study: Conscientious Objectors

Have a go at the activities below to help you understand how the treatment of conscientious objectors changed between the First World War and the Second World War, and why these changes happened.

Knowledge and Understanding

1) In your own words, describe the Military Service Act and explain why it was introduced. Give as much detail as possible.

2) Explain what a conscientious objector is.

3) Copy and complete the mind map below by explaining the reasons why people became conscientious objectors in the First World War.

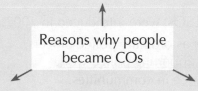

Reasons why people became COs

4) Explain the role of the Central Board of Conscientious Objectors.

Thinking Historically

1) Copy and complete the table below, describing the treatment of conscientious objectors in the First and Second World Wars by each group in the table. Give as much detail as possible.

Group	Response in WW1	Response in WW2
a) **The government**		
b) **Members of the public**		
c) **The British Army**		

2) Do you think the treatment of conscientious objectors changed significantly between the First and Second World Wars? Explain your answer?

3) Explain the similarities between the way conscientious objectors were treated by the government in the 20th century and the way the Tolpuddle Martyrs were treated by the government in the 19th century. Use the information on pages 40 and 58 to help you.

EXAM TIP

Many people conscientiously objected to COs...

You might be asked to explain why an aspect of crime and punishment changed quickly or slowly. You'll need to write about the factors that might have affected the speed of that change.

Crime and Punishment in Modern Britain, c.1900-present

Changes in Law Enforcement

Methods used by the police to catch criminals and prevent crime have changed a lot since 1900.

Community Policing has changed the way the law is Enforced

Over the last fifty years, policing in the UK has become more focused on crime prevention through the use of community policing.

The Neighbourhood Watch was first established in the UK in 1982.
* The Neighbourhood Watch scheme encourages local people to work together with the police to keep communities safe by reporting suspicious behaviour and sharing information.
* However, only a small minority of households in England and Wales are covered by the scheme (around 3.8 million).

Police Community Support Officers (PCSOs) were introduced in 2002.
* PCSOs don't have the same powers as ordinary police officers, but they play an important role in supporting police work and acting as a visible police presence in communities.
* One of the main roles of a PCSO is to patrol a beat and interact with the public. This was traditionally the role of ordinary police constables, but changes to government policy mean fewer officers are doing this work.

Comment and Analysis

Encouraging local people to help police the community is not a new development — local people have had a role in policing since the Anglo-Saxon period (see p.8). However, members of the community are no longer expected to capture criminals.

Bright signs are usually used to mark out Neighbourhood Watch areas.

The Training and Organisation of the police has changed

1) In 1900, the training of police officers was basic. A National Police College was established in 1947 to teach recruits the skills required for the role. Today, recruits are trained through the College of Policing.

2) Specialist units are now common. These include Firearms Units, Counter Terrorism Units, Dog-Handling Units and Forensic Services. This means there are highly trained units to deal with specific emergencies.

3) Some changes have made it easier for different police forces to work together. The number of local police forces has been reduced since 1900 to 43 to help each police force work more effectively. Records are now stored centrally and information is shared between police forces.

Advances in Technology have changed how the police work

1) Forensics (using scientific tests to investigate crime) were used in the 20th century to link criminals to crimes. In 1902, fingerprint evidence was used to convict a criminal for the first time. Other forensic developments include bloodstain pattern analysis and the use of DNA to identify suspects.

2) Over the last 150 years, the police have used a variety of new forms of transport to allow them to travel more quickly and pursue suspects. These include bicycles, cars, speed boats and helicopters.

3) Advances in communication technology have allowed the police to better coordinate their activities.

In the 1920s, the police began using Morse Code transmitters and special police telephone boxes so that officers could call for help.

In the 1930s, two-way radios were first installed in police cars, while the 999 system was set up for the public to make emergency calls.

4) Computer systems have improved over the past fifty years, leading to better record keeping and collaboration between forces. The Police National Computer was created in 1974, providing a database for information such as DNA and fingerprint records, or details of wanted criminals and missing persons.

5) CCTV is used by the police to track criminal activity and identify suspects.

6) Police officers now use a range of equipment to protect themselves and help them arrest criminals. This includes body armour, weapons that use electric currents to stun criminals, CS gas (tear gas) and the traditional truncheon used by police since the 1800s. Some specialist police officers also carry firearms.

Changes in Law Enforcement

Give these activities a go to check that you know all of the changes to modern-day law enforcement.

Knowledge and Understanding

1) Describe how each of the following contributes to community policing:

> a) The Neighbourhood Watch scheme

> b) Police Community Support Officers

2) Describe one difference between the role of the local community in policing in the Anglo-Saxon period and the role of the local community in policing today.

3) In your own words, describe how the training of police officers has changed since the start of the 20th century.

Thinking Historically

1) Explain why science and technology have been important in the development of law enforcement since 1900. Include the following key words in your explanation.

> forensics transport communication technology computer systems CCTV weapons

2) Copy and complete the table below, adding information about each aspect of policing in the different time periods identified. Use the information on pages 26, 48, 50 and 60 to help you.

Aspect of policing	c.1500-c.1700	c.1700-c.1900	c.1900-present
a) **Purpose**			
b) **Organisation**			
c) **Training**			
d) **Methods**			

3) In which of the time periods in the table above do you think there was the most significant change to policing? Explain your answer.

There are just so many ways to catch a criminal...

There are many examples of the role of technology in law enforcement — e.g. the use of Morse Code transmitters. Don't just name examples though — explain why they're important.

Crime and Punishment in Modern Britain, c.1900-present

The Death Penalty

During the 20th century, use of the <u>death penalty</u> in Britain <u>declined</u> until it was finally <u>abolished</u> in the <u>1960s</u>.

Some 20th-century Politicians argued Against the Death Penalty

1) In the 1920s, groups like the <u>Howard League</u> and the <u>National Council for the Abolition of the Death Penalty</u> began campaigning against <u>capital punishment</u> in Britain. They were known as <u>abolitionists</u>. Some <u>politicians</u> were in favour of abolition, so the issue began to be <u>debated</u> in Parliament.

Arguments for the Death Penalty

- Death was seen as the ultimate <u>deterrent</u>, convincing others not to <u>commit murder</u>.
- <u>Executing</u> murderers was the only way to ensure that they could no longer be a <u>threat to society</u>.
- It was <u>more expensive</u> to punish murderers with <u>life imprisonment</u> than it was to <u>execute</u> them.
- Some murders were seen as so <u>appalling</u> that death was the only way for society to get <u>retribution</u>.

Arguments against the Death Penalty

- Execution wasn't really seen as a <u>deterrent</u> by some — murders continued to happen despite the death penalty. It didn't prevent <u>unplanned killings</u>.
- Many felt that execution was an <u>uncivilised</u> way for society to deal with criminals because it went against their <u>religious</u> or <u>moral principles</u>.
- In countries where the death penalty was no longer used, murder <u>hadn't increased</u>. <u>Sweden</u> abolished it in <u>1921</u>, but the murder rate hadn't risen.
- The legal system could make <u>mistakes</u> and execute an <u>innocent</u> person.

> In <u>1930</u>, there wasn't enough support in <u>Parliament</u> for the <u>suspension</u> of the death penalty, as it was thought that most members of the <u>public supported</u> capital punishment. The issue was also considered <u>less important</u> than other social issues at the time.

2) Politicians tried to <u>suspend</u> capital punishment for a <u>trial period</u> in the 1930s, but their attempts <u>failed</u>. However, the execution of <u>pregnant women</u> and people <u>under 18</u> was <u>banned</u> in the early 1930s. Execution of <u>under 16s</u> had been banned in <u>1908</u>, and no one under 18 had been hanged since <u>1889</u>.

Efforts to Abolish the Death Penalty were Renewed in the 1940s

1) In 1948, MPs in the <u>House of Commons</u> voted to <u>suspend</u> the <u>death penalty</u>, but the <u>House of Lords</u> didn't support them so it was <u>retained</u>. <u>Public opinion</u> was still strongly <u>in favour</u> of the death penalty.

2) A <u>Royal Commission</u> was set up in 1949 to look into whether laws about <u>capital punishment</u> should be changed. In 1953, the Commission recommended <u>changing the law</u> to remove the death penalty for those <u>under 21</u> and the <u>mentally ill</u>, but they didn't recommend <u>abolition</u> unless the <u>public</u> wanted it.

3) Several high profile cases in the 1950s highlighted <u>issues</u> with the death penalty:

> In <u>1950</u>, <u>Timothy Evans</u> was hanged for killing his wife and child. He insisted during his trial that a man named <u>John Christie</u> had committed the murders. Three years later, evidence emerged suggesting that Christie was the <u>real murderer</u>.

> <u>Ruth Ellis</u> was hanged in <u>1955</u> for killing her abusive boyfriend. The public <u>sympathised</u> with Ellis because she had been <u>abused</u> by her victim — her execution received a lot of <u>negative coverage</u> in the press.

> Nineteen-year-old <u>Derek Bentley</u> was executed for the murder of a policeman in 1953, even though he <u>hadn't actually fired the gun</u> that killed the policeman (see p.64).

4) However, the <u>public</u> remained in favour of <u>capital punishment</u> in the 1950s and 1960s — many feared that <u>murder rates</u> would increase if the <u>deterrent</u> of execution was removed. Despite this, <u>politicians</u> were increasingly in favour of <u>abolition</u>. They eventually <u>passed laws</u> to <u>abolish capital punishment</u>.

- The <u>1957 Homicide Act</u> introduced different punishments for different categories of murder. Only the <u>worst</u> kinds of murders were now punishable by <u>execution</u>.
- In <u>1965</u>, MPs passed the <u>Murder (Abolition of Death Penalty) Act</u>, which <u>suspended</u> capital punishment in Britain. In <u>1969</u>, the death penalty was permanently <u>abolished</u>.

Comment and Analysis

While some politicians <u>shared</u> the views of the public on capital punishment, other politicians were <u>strongly against</u> the death penalty. They <u>ignored</u> public opinion and <u>followed</u> their own <u>conscience</u>.

The Death Penalty

Try these activities to check that you know how the death penalty was eventually abolished.

Knowledge and Understanding

1) Copy and complete the mind map below, giving reasons why people in the 20th century thought the death penalty should be used and reasons why people thought it shouldn't be used.

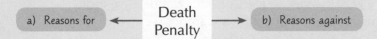

a) Reasons for ← Death Penalty → b) Reasons against

2) Explain how the law was changed in 1908 to protect young people.

3) Copy and complete the timeline below by filling in the developments in the decline of the death penalty between the 1920s and 1969. Include as much detail as you can.

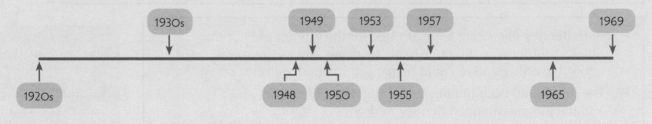

1930s   1949   1953   1957   1969

1920s   1948 1950 1955   1965

Thinking Historically

1) Explain how the government's attitude towards the death penalty changed between the early modern period and the 20th century. Use the information on pages 28, 42 and 62 to help you.

2) Copy and complete the table below by explaining how each factor affected the movement to abolish the death penalty in the 20th century.

Factor	Impact on the abolitionist movement
a) The government	
b) Public attitudes	
c) Abolition groups	

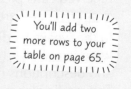

You'll add two more rows to your table on page 65.

3) Why do you think it took several decades for the death penalty to be fully abolished in the 20th century? Use your answers to question 2 to help you explain your answer.

EXAM TIP

The death penalty was also abolished in football...

To hit the top marks on the last question of the paper, you need to go beyond the prompts given in the question. You can use these as a starting point, but write about other factors too.

Crime and Punishment in Modern Britain, c.1900-present

Case Study: The Derek Bentley Case

The case of Derek Bentley had a significant impact on public attitudes towards the death penalty.

Derek Bentley was Executed for Murder in 1953

In 1952, Derek Bentley was sentenced to death for a murder that was committed by his accomplice.

- In November 1952, 19-year-old Derek Bentley and 16-year-old Christopher Craig attempted to burgle a warehouse.
- During the burglary, the police arrived and cornered them on the roof. Bentley was detained by Detective Sergeant Frederick Fairfax.
- There are conflicting reports of what happened next. According to the witness statements of three policemen, Bentley broke free and shouted to Craig, 'Let him have it, Chris'. Both Craig and Bentley later denied that Bentley said this.
- At this point, Craig fired his gun, injuring DS Fairfax. As more police officers arrived, Craig continued to shoot at them. During the shooting, PC Sidney Miles was killed.

> Derek Bentley was illiterate (he couldn't read or write properly) and he was thought to have a mental age of about 11. This evidence might have affected the sentence he received, but it was not made available to the jury at his trial.

- Both Bentley and Craig were arrested for the murder of PC Sidney Miles. Murder was still punishable by death, but as Craig was under 18, only Bentley could be hanged if found guilty.
- The jury found both Bentley and Craig guilty of murder and the judge sentenced Bentley to death.
- The Home Secretary could have recommended that the Queen use her 'royal prerogative of mercy' to allow Bentley to go to prison instead, but he decided that there was no reason to do so. Attempts to overturn the decision were unsuccessful and Bentley was hanged in January 1953.

> Much of the trial focused on the phrase 'Let him have it'. The jury were told that the phrase showed 'common purpose' meaning that both Bentley and Craig wanted the police officer to be killed. The lawyers defending Bentley argued that Bentley meant 'Give him the gun' rather than 'Shoot him'.

The case had a Huge Impact on Attitudes to the Death Penalty

1) Before the execution, 200 MPs signed a petition calling for Bentley to be reprieved, meaning he wouldn't receive the death penalty, but the case couldn't be discussed in Parliament until after the execution.

2) MPs received many protests from their constituents, and the Home Office received calls pleading for mercy in the build up to the execution. Bentley's supporters gathered around Parliament and outside the prison he was held in.

3) In the weeks leading up to the execution, members of Bentley's family were interviewed by the media. Their desperate pleas for his life and descriptions of his low intelligence were widely publicised. The media also presented widespread coverage of the public protests.

4) Following the execution, Bentley's relatives started a campaign to clear his name. This kept the case in the public eye and convinced many that the justice system in Britain had major failings.

A photograph of Derek Bentley

Comment and Analysis

Bentley's learning difficulties and the fact that it was Craig who had pulled the trigger made this a significant case. Along with the cases of Timothy Evans and Ruth Ellis (see p.62), it caused both members of the public and politicians to reconsider existing laws about capital punishment. The 1957 Homicide Act and the other changes that followed were partly responses to these high profile cases.

> Some people believe that Bentley was refused a pardon because the government wanted to make an example of him at a time when violence towards police officers was becoming increasingly common. This suggested that the justice system was failing because the death penalty could be misused.

Case Study: The Derek Bentley Case

The Derek Bentley case played an important role in abolishing the death penalty. These activities will help you understand why attitudes towards the death penalty changed as a result of this case.

Knowledge and Understanding

1) Copy and complete the flowchart below, adding the missing information about the events of the Derek Bentley case.

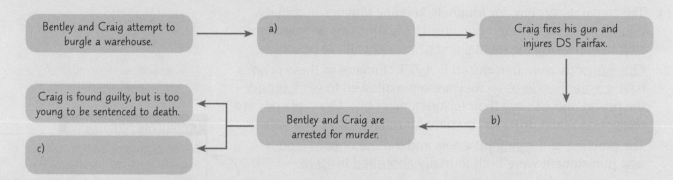

| Bentley and Craig attempt to burgle a warehouse. | → | a) | → | Craig fires his gun and injures DS Fairfax. |

| Craig is found guilty, but is too young to be sentenced to death. | ← | Bentley and Craig are arrested for murder. | ← | b) |

c)

2) In your own words, explain why the phrase 'Let him have it' was important in the case.

3) Copy and complete the table below, explaining how each of the following people reacted to Derek Bentley's sentence.

People	Reaction
a) The Home Secretary	
b) MPs	
c) Bentley's family	
d) The public	

Thinking Historically

1) On page 63, you made a table of different factors that had an impact on the movement to abolish the death penalty. Complete your table by adding a row for each of the factors below.

High profile cases   The media

The Bentley case was a wake-up call for many people...

In Paper 1, Section B, you'll only need to answer one of questions 5 or 6 — don't answer both questions. You should pick the question you feel you can give the strongest answer for.

Crime and Punishment in Modern Britain, c.1900-present

The Modern Prison System

Since the end of the 19th century, the British prison system has been changed to help prisoners reform.

Modern Prisons aim to Rehabilitate and Reform offenders

After the 1865 Prisons Act was passed, life in prisons became very harsh (see p.46). However, in 1895 a parliamentary committee called the Gladstone Committee published a report recommending that British prisons should aim to reform offenders as well as deterring them from committing more crimes. Over the next century, changes made to the prison system reflected this renewed focus on rehabilitation.

1) The 'separate system' for routinely keeping inmates in solitary confinement was phased out after 1922. This was an important step in improving the mental and physical health of prisoners.

2) Open prisons were introduced in 1933. Inmates in these prisons have greater freedoms — they are often allowed to work outside the prison and can use their leisure time freely. Open prisons are designed to help prisoners prepare for reintegration into society.

3) The practice of flogging prisoners and the use of hard labour as a punishment were both formally abolished in 1948.

4) Modern prisons focus on reducing re-offending rates by providing inmates with education and skills. Prisoners' living conditions have improved as a result — prisoners today receive a good diet and healthcare, and have the right to be treated with dignity.

Since 1900, the number of inmates in UK prisons has grown significantly. This has caused overcrowding, which can result in worse living conditions for prisoners.

Comment and Analysis

In the 20th century, there was a renewed focus on the ideas of the early 19th century that prison should be used to reform criminals (see p.44). This change in perspective has changed the way modern prisons operate.

There are now several Alternatives to Prison

In the 20th century, various schemes were introduced to reform criminals by keeping them away from prison.

1) Probation was officially introduced in 1907 — offenders on probation can serve part of their sentence outside of prison. They have to regularly meet a probation officer, whose job is to help them to reform.

2) Since 1967, some offenders have been allowed to leave prison on parole after serving a certain amount of their sentence. This means that well-behaved offenders can leave prison early as long as they agree to certain conditions. This was designed to reduce the number of inmates in prisons, as well as helping to rehabilitate prisoners and giving them a chance to reintegrate into society before finishing their sentence.

3) Community Service Orders were introduced in 1972 for people who have committed a crime for the first time or who have committed minor crimes. Community service might involve getting rid of graffiti or picking up litter.

4) Some punishments aim to rehabilitate criminals by encouraging them to change their lifestyle. Monitoring methods like electronic tagging can be used instead of prison, and restorative justice allows offenders to meet their victims and see the impact of their crimes.

Electronic tagging involves offenders being made to wear a tag around their ankle so that police know where they are. Criminal Behaviour Orders replaced Anti-Social Behaviour Orders in 2014. They are designed to control what an offender can and can't do.

Young Offenders were Treated Differently after 1900

1) In the 1800s, the law began to treat child and adult offenders differently. For example, from the 1850s, children could be sent to reformatory schools instead of prison. In 1895, the Gladstone Committee recommended that young offenders between the ages of 16 and 21 should also be treated differently.

2) The Committee suggested that young offenders should be imprisoned separately from adult offenders. After a successful trial period, the first borstal (a type of youth detention centre) was opened in 1902.

3) In 1908, the first juvenile courts were established — children were now tried separately from adults.

4) The age at which a child can be found guilty of a crime in Britain was raised from 7 to 8 in 1933. This age of criminal responsibility was raised again to 10 in 1963 (but only in England and Wales). The government made these changes to protect children from being unfairly treated as adults.

The Modern Prison System

Get these changes to the modern prison system stuck in your head with the activities on the page below.

Knowledge and Understanding

1) Use the information on the previous page to write a definition for each of the following terms:

    a) Gladstone Committee   c) reformatory school   e) open prison

    b) restorative justice   d) borstal

2) Copy and complete the table below by adding as much detail as possible about each of these alternatives to prison.

Probation	Parole	Community Service Orders

Thinking Historically

1) Copy and complete the mind map below, giving as much detail as you can about the purpose of prisons in each time period. You can use the information on pages 44, 46, 50 and 66 to help you.

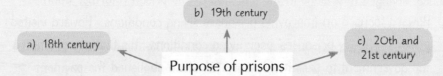

b) 19th century

a) 18th century

Purpose of prisons

c) 20th and 21st century

2) 'There were significant changes to how criminals were punished in the period c.1900-present.' Use the table to help you structure each paragraph of an essay explaining how far you agree with this view.

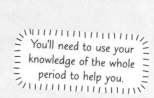

You'll need to use your knowledge of the whole period to help you.

Point	Evidence	Why evidence supports point?
The end of corporal punishment in prisons was a significant turning point in how criminals were punished.	The practice of flogging and the use of hard labour as a punishment were both abolished in 1948. Corporal punishment had been used in Britain since the Anglo-Saxon period.	The end of corporal punishment represented a significant change because it ended the use of physical violence as a punishment, which had been a key method of deterring criminals in earlier periods.

Add three rows to the table to plan three more paragraphs.

Make sure you write points that agree and disagree with the statement.

Talk about different types of punishment and how far they changed.

Prison life improved a great deal...

When you're planning longer answers, jot down examples and relevant information that will help you to back up each point you want to make. This will help you support your argument.

Worked Exam-Style Question

The sample answer below will help you to answer the 16-mark question in the exam.

'The desire to improve conditions for prisoners has been the main reason for changes to prisons since c.1700.'

Explain how far you agree with this statement.

You could mention:
- Elizabeth Fry
- open prisons

You should also use your own knowledge.   [16 marks]

For questions like this in the exam, 4 extra marks will be awarded for spelling, punctuation, grammar and using specialist terminology.

It's a good idea to include a short introduction summarising your argument.

I do not agree that the desire to improve conditions for prisoners has been the main reason for changes to prisons since c.1700. Although the desire to improve prison conditions had a major influence on changes to prisons in the late 18th century and early 19th century, changing attitudes towards the purpose of prisons have had a more significant influence on changes to prisons since then.

This paragraph explains why the desire to improve conditions has been significant.

The desire to improve conditions for prisoners was an important reason for changes to prisons in the late 1700s. The prison reformer John Howard focused on improving prisoners' living conditions. Howard visited prisons to study prisoners' poor living conditions. His findings prompted the government to pass two Acts in 1774 which abolished the payment of jailer's fees and required all prisons to provide a safe and hygienic environment for prisoners, including access to medical care. The changes brought in by these Acts were directly motivated by the desire to improve living conditions in prisons.

Use specific and relevant examples to support your points.

Explain how the reason given in the question had an impact on changing prisons.

The desire to improve conditions for prisoners remained an important reason for changes to prisons in the early 19th century. Elizabeth Fry worked to improve the conditions for female prisoners at Newgate Prison and campaigned for changes to prisons across the country. Several of her suggestions, such as the separation of male and female prisoners and the introduction of female jailers, were included in Robert Peel's 1823 Gaols Act, which aimed to improve conditions for prisoners across the country.

Include specific dates to show you have a good knowledge of the period.

However, since the early 19th century, changing attitudes about the purpose of prisons have been a more important reason for changes to prisons. The Prison Act of 1839 was partly motivated by a desire to improve conditions for prisoners. For example, it led to the creation of Pentonville Prison, which was designed to provide better living conditions

Even if you agree with the statement, it's important to consider both sides of the argument.

You need to show you know the order of events.

Crime and Punishment in Modern Britain, c.1900-present

Worked Exam-Style Question

than many of the existing prisons in Britain. However, the Act was also motivated by the growing support for the idea that prisons should help to rehabilitate prisoners. As a result, prisons like Pentonville used the 'separate system', which was intended to reform prisoners by isolating them from each other so they had time to reflect on their crimes. This shows that there was a move towards changing prisons to focus on reforming prisoners, rather than simply improving conditions for them.

> Explain how each point you make is relevant to the question.

> Start a new paragraph every time you introduce a new point.

Changing attitudes about the purpose of prisons were also the main reason for changes to prisons in the second half of the 19th century. Many people at this time believed there was a 'criminal class' of lifelong criminals who were incapable of being reformed. Others thought that conditions in prisons weren't harsh enough because prisons weren't succeeding at deterring criminals. A combination of these ideas led to the passing of the 1865 Prisons Act, which made conditions in prisons worse in an effort to punish prisoners more harshly. The fact that conditions were made deliberately worse emphasises that the desire to improve conditions in prisons played no role in these changes.

> Remember to explain the significance of each reason you write about.

Changing attitudes about the purpose of prison have also been the main reason for change in the modern period. There has been a renewed focus on rehabilitating prisoners, as well as preparing them for reintegration into society. For example, open prisons were introduced in 1933. Inmates in these prisons are permitted to work outside the prison and can choose how to spend their leisure time, with the aim of preparing them for reintegration into society. Although some changes in the modern period, such as the abolition of hard labour in prisons in 1948, have improved living conditions for prisoners, changes in this period were mainly motivated by the idea that prisons should aim to rehabilitate prisoners.

> You should include examples throughout your answer.

In conclusion, the desire to improve conditions for prisoners has not been the main reason for changes to prisons since c.1700. It was an important reason for prison reform in the 18th century and the beginning of the 19th century, but changing attitudes about the purpose of prisons have been a more important reason since the passing of the Prison Act of 1839. Although prison conditions improved as a result of many of the changes introduced after 1839, these reforms were motivated by the development of different ideas about how prisons should function.

> Make sure you give a clear answer to the question in your conclusion.

> Summarise your argument in your conclusion.

Crime and Punishment in Modern Britain, c.1900-present

Exam-Style Questions

Give these exam-style questions a go to test your knowledge of modern crime and punishment. Remember that you might need to include details about crime and punishment from earlier periods too.

Exam-Style Questions

1) Explain one similarity between local law enforcement in the early modern period (c.1500-c.1700) and in the modern period (c.1900-present).   [4 marks]

2) Explain why the use of capital punishment changed significantly in the 20th century.

   You could mention:
   • abolitionists
   • Derek Bentley

   You should also use your own knowledge.   [12 marks]

3) 'Changing social attitudes have been the main factor in changing definitions of crime in the modern period (c.1900-present).'

   Explain how far you agree with this statement.

   You could mention:
   • decriminalisation
   • car-related crime

   For the 16-mark question in the exam, 4 extra marks will be available for spelling, punctuation, grammar and using specialist terminology.

   You should also use your own knowledge.   [16 marks]

Exam-Style Questions

Exam-Style Questions

4) Explain one difference between the purpose of punishment in the early modern period (c.1500-c.1700) and in the modern period (c.1900-present).　　[4 marks]

5) Explain why there were developments in the crime of theft in the period c.1700-present.

   You could mention:
   • highway robbery
   • computers

   You should also use your own knowledge.　　[12 marks]

6) 'The role of individuals has been the most important factor in the development of policing since c.1700.'

   Explain how far you agree with this statement.

   You could mention:
   • Robert Peel
   • communication technology

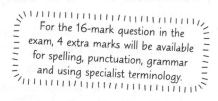
For the 16-mark question in the exam, 4 extra marks will be available for spelling, punctuation, grammar and using specialist terminology.

   You should also use your own knowledge.　　[16 marks]

Housing and Employment

The <u>Historic Environment</u> part of your exam will be about <u>Whitechapel</u> between around <u>1870</u> and <u>1900</u>. Whitechapel was a part of <u>East London</u>, and its <u>features</u> had an impact on <u>crime</u> and <u>policing</u> in the area.

Whitechapel was Rundown and Overcrowded

© Chronicle / Alamy Stock Photo

Whitechapel was <u>very densely populated</u> in the late 1800s. In 1881, more than <u>30,000</u> people lived in around <u>3500</u> homes. This meant the area was very <u>overcrowded</u>.

1) There were lots of <u>small</u>, <u>dark streets</u> and <u>alleyways</u>, and many people lived in <u>slums</u> called '<u>rookeries</u>'. These were <u>crowded areas</u> of <u>low-quality housing</u>. Some rookery buildings were <u>several storeys high</u>, and <u>over thirty people</u> might share <u>one house</u> or <u>apartment</u>.

An artist's impression of a street in Whitechapel in 1870.

2) Some people lived in <u>lodging houses</u> called <u>doss houses</u>, where individuals could sleep on <u>dormitory-style</u> bunks for just a <u>few pence</u> a night. Lodgers could pay a <u>cheaper price</u> if they slept <u>upright</u> and <u>leaning</u> over a <u>rope</u>.

3) Other people had to live in <u>workhouses</u>, which offered free accommodation to the very <u>young</u>, <u>old</u>, <u>poor</u> or <u>chronically ill</u>, who might otherwise be on the <u>streets</u>. Workhouses were <u>unpleasant</u> — the <u>accommodation</u> was of a <u>poor standard</u>, <u>discipline</u> was <u>harsh</u> and <u>families</u> were often <u>split up</u>. Those who could <u>work</u> spent <u>long hours</u> doing <u>repetitive tasks</u> like <u>picking apart old rope</u> to earn their keep.

4) Many of those who lived in Whitechapel <u>couldn't afford</u> to move to an area with <u>better housing</u>.

The Government tried to Improve Housing in Whitechapel

1) In 1875, parliament passed the <u>Artisans' Dwellings Act</u> in an attempt to <u>clear</u> some of the <u>worst slums</u> in the country and replace them with <u>better housing</u>.

2) One area of Whitechapel that was particularly <u>rundown</u> was sold to a charity called the <u>Peabody Trust</u>. The Trust built <u>eleven new blocks of flats</u> that contained a total of <u>286 apartments</u>. This was called the <u>Peabody Estate</u>.

Comment and Analysis

The establishment of the Estate <u>didn't improve</u> housing in Whitechapel <u>as a whole</u>. The changes were only in <u>one small area</u>, and many families there were <u>unable</u> to rent the new apartments due to their <u>high cost</u>. This meant they had to move <u>elsewhere</u>, adding to <u>overcrowding</u> in other parts of Whitechapel.

The apartments were called '<u>model dwellings</u>'. They were meant to provide <u>better living conditions</u> than those in existing housing in the area, with <u>more living space</u> and shared <u>yards</u> and <u>laundry facilities</u>. However, the <u>rent</u> was <u>higher</u> than most Whitechapel residents could afford.

Poverty and Crime were Common in Whitechapel

1) People in Whitechapel typically <u>didn't have much money</u>. <u>Unemployment</u> in the area was <u>high</u> — lots of people <u>struggled</u> to find a job. Even if they managed to get a job, it would often only provide work for <u>a few days</u> before <u>another period</u> of unemployment.

2) Many of those who did have a job worked as <u>labourers</u> for <u>low wages</u>.

3) Poverty and poor housing also caused <u>health issues</u> for some residents of Whitechapel. <u>Diseases</u> like diphtheria and dysentery <u>spread easily</u> in the <u>overcrowded slums</u>, and not having enough to <u>eat</u> due to <u>lack of money</u> meant people were <u>less likely</u> to be able to <u>fight off</u> illness.

4) These issues related to work and poverty caused high rates of <u>discontent</u> and <u>desperation</u> among Whitechapel residents:

- <u>Alcoholism</u> was common, as people tried to use alcohol to <u>escape</u> their <u>hard life</u>.

- Some people also became involved in <u>crime</u> as a way to <u>make money</u>.

- The shortage of jobs also led some women to become <u>prostitutes</u>. Prostitution could be <u>dangerous</u> (see p.78), but for some it was the <u>only way to survive</u>.

There's more on the links between <u>Whitechapel's environment</u> and <u>crime</u> on p.74.

Housing and Employment

Living conditions in Whitechapel at the end of the 19th century were very poor. Use the activities on this page to improve your knowledge of the different problems that were caused by poverty and unemployment.

Knowledge and Understanding

1) Describe the key features of each of the following types of housing:
   a) A rookery
   b) A doss house
   c) A workhouse

2) Using your own words, explain why the construction of the Peabody Estate didn't create better living conditions in Whitechapel as a whole.

3) Copy and complete the mind map below, explaining as many of the effects of unemployment and poverty experienced by the people of Whitechapel as you can. Add as much detail as you can.

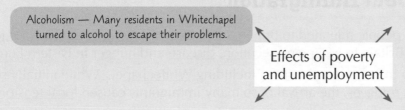

Alcoholism — Many residents in Whitechapel turned to alcohol to escape their problems.

Effects of poverty and unemployment

Source Analysis

The source below is an extract from an article about overcrowding in Whitechapel, published in the London newspaper *Pall Mall Gazette* on the 28th February 1870.

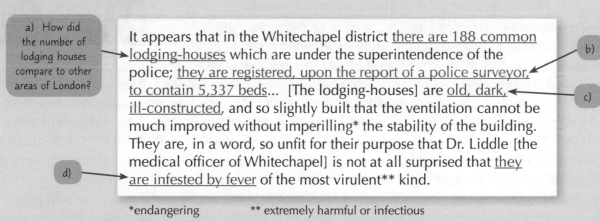

a) How did the number of lodging houses compare to other areas of London?

It appears that in the Whitechapel district there are 188 common lodging-houses which are under the superintendence of the police; they are registered, upon the report of a police surveyor, to contain 5,337 beds... [The lodging-houses] are old, dark, ill-constructed, and so slightly built that the ventilation cannot be much improved without imperilling* the stability of the building. They are, in a word, so unfit for their purpose that Dr. Liddle [the medical officer of Whitechapel] is not at all surprised that they are infested by fever of the most virulent** kind.

b)

c)

d)

*endangering   ** extremely harmful or infectious

1) Some details in the source have been highlighted. For each detail, write down a question you could ask to find out more about living conditions in Whitechapel in around 1870. The first one has been done for you.

2) Give an example of a kind of source that might help you to answer each of the questions above. Explain how the source would help you to answer the question.

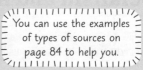

You can use the examples of types of sources on page 84 to help you.

EXAM TIP

Overcrowding can be a problem when you're trying to write a book...

The first question in the exam is all about describing features. To get full marks, make sure you identify two separate features and give a piece of supporting information about each one.

Social Tensions

In the late 1800s in Whitechapel, <u>high levels</u> of <u>poverty</u> and <u>insecure housing</u> affected people's sense of <u>community</u>. The growth of <u>immigration</u>, <u>socialism</u> and <u>anarchism</u> created even more <u>tension</u> in the area.

The Population of Whitechapel was Constantly Changing

Many people in Whitechapel slept in different <u>lodging houses</u> each night, or on the <u>street</u>. <u>Pubs</u> attracted people from outside the area to <u>stay</u>, <u>eat</u> or <u>drink</u>, as well as <u>prostitutes</u> looking for clients, and <u>thieves</u> looking for victims. Those who did live in one place <u>wouldn't have the same neighbours</u> for very long.

Having lots of different people <u>moving in and out</u> of the area might have made it easier to <u>commit crime</u>. <u>Community ties</u> were often <u>weak</u>, which meant people <u>didn't know</u> their neighbours very well and were <u>less likely</u> to <u>look out</u> for them. <u>Lodgers</u> also had to <u>carry their possessions</u> with them every day, making them <u>targets</u> for <u>thieves</u>.

→ This changing population also made it harder for the police to <u>investigate crimes</u> as people did not <u>stay in the same place</u> for long. By the next day, key <u>witnesses</u> to a crime might have <u>moved on</u>.

People were Unhappy about Immigration

1) In the late 19th century, lots of <u>Irish</u> people <u>migrated to Britain</u>, often to avoid <u>famine</u> or to look for <u>jobs</u>. Many <u>Jewish</u> people also moved to Britain to <u>escape persecution</u>, <u>disease</u> and <u>hunger</u> in Eastern Europe.

2) Many of these immigrants ended up in <u>poor</u> areas of <u>cities</u>, including <u>Whitechapel</u>. While initially some people had <u>sympathy</u> for the <u>Jewish refugees</u>, the arrival of so many immigrants caused <u>local tensions</u>.

Reactions to Immigration in Whitechapel

- Some Whitechapel residents worried that immigrants were taking <u>jobs</u>. Immigrants would work for <u>low pay</u>, with many Jewish people employed in <u>sweatshops</u> — <u>small, unregulated factories</u> where they worked for <u>long hours</u> and <u>little money</u>. Some British workers felt this <u>undercut wages</u>.

- Immigrants rented <u>homes</u> in Whitechapel, <u>adding</u> to <u>existing overcrowding</u> (see p.72). This caused <u>resentment</u> among some in Whitechapel.

- Some immigrants experienced <u>racism</u>, or were <u>unfairly targeted</u> by the <u>police</u>. <u>Media portrayals</u> of immigrants were often <u>negative</u> and <u>stereotypical</u>, e.g. Irish people were <u>stereotyped</u> as <u>violent</u> or <u>drunk</u>.

An engraving of Petticoat Lane Market in Whitechapel, where many Jewish vendors worked, from the 1870s.

- Many Jewish immigrants lived on <u>just a few streets</u> in Whitechapel, which meant they were <u>segregated</u> (separated from other people). This reduced interaction between them and existing residents, which made it easier for existing residents to <u>believe stereotypes</u> about them. Jewish people also had their <u>own language and customs</u>, which made some local people <u>distrust</u> them.

- Some immigrants were involved in <u>crime</u>, e.g. a number of <u>gangs</u> in Whitechapel (see p.78) were made up of <u>newcomers</u> who targeted other immigrants and Whitechapel residents, creating <u>fear</u>.

- In the 1880s, several <u>bomb attacks</u> occurred in London, carried out by certain supporters of <u>Irish independence</u> called <u>Fenians</u>. People's <u>anger</u> about the attacks was often directed at <u>Irish immigrants</u>.

Socialism and Anarchism were On The Rise

In the late 1800s, <u>socialism</u> and <u>anarchism</u> were becoming <u>increasingly popular</u> in Europe. Socialism is a belief that everyone is <u>equal</u> and that <u>money</u> and <u>property</u> should be <u>shared equally</u>. Anarchists believe there should be <u>no formal government</u> and people in society should work together <u>voluntarily</u>.

1) <u>Whitechapel</u> saw an increase in people supporting <u>socialism</u> and <u>anarchism</u> at this time. Some of these ideas developed in <u>other countries</u>, including <u>Russia</u> — their growth in Whitechapel is partly explained by the arrival of <u>Jewish</u> immigrants who were <u>familiar</u> with these ideas from <u>Eastern Europe</u>.

2) There were some <u>concerns</u> that these movements would <u>disrupt social order</u>. People would also often accuse <u>Jewish immigrants</u> of <u>links</u> to socialism and anarchism and <u>blame</u> them for their problems. Some Jewish immigrants did have <u>radical beliefs</u> and set up <u>socialist organisations</u> and <u>newspapers</u>.

Social Tensions

Have a go at the activities below about the social tensions in Whitechapel and the reasons for them.

Source Analysis

The sources below show attitudes towards Jewish immigrants in Whitechapel in 1889.

Source A

Source A is a cartoon published in *The English Illustrated Magazine* in 1889. The text reads 'Jew Traders in Petticoat Lane — "Here ye are! Here ye are! Any price you like! I don't care!"' Source B is an extract from a survey of poverty in London published in 1889 by Charles Booth, a researcher and social reformer. He visited Whitechapel and other areas of London over many years to carry out his survey.

Source B
Whitechapel is... a gathering together of poor fortune seekers; its streets are full of buying and selling, the poor living on the poor. Here, just outside the old City walls, have always lived the Jews, and here they are now in thousands, both old established and new comers, seeking their livelihood under conditions which seem to suit them on the middle ground between civilization and barbarism.

1) Copy and complete the table by explaining how the author and purpose of Source A influence its usefulness for an investigation into attitudes towards Jewish immigrants in Whitechapel.

Feature	Usefulness
a) Content	The source is useful because it shows that people believed Jewish traders were untrustworthy and sold their produce at suspiciously low prices to win custom. Its usefulness is limited because it refers specifically to Jewish traders rather than all Jewish immigrants.
b) Author	
c) Purpose	

2) Make another copy of the table above. Fill it in by explaining how the content, author and purpose of Source B affect its usefulness for an investigation into attitudes towards Jewish immigrants in Whitechapel.

Knowledge and Understanding

1) Explain why the constant movement of people around Whitechapel contributed to crime in the area and made it harder to catch criminals.

2) Explain why some people living in Whitechapel in the late 19th century blamed immigrants for each of the problems below. Give as much detail as you can.

a) Unemployment   b) Overcrowding   c) Crime   d) The growth of socialism and anarchism

Immigration — an easy scapegoat for people's problems...
When writing about the usefulness of a source, it's important to think about how the source's context affects its usefulness. Use your own knowledge of the period to back up your points.

Whitechapel, c.1870-c.1900

Policing in the Late 19th Century

Crime in London was handled by the Metropolitan Police. The force changed a lot in the 1800s.

The Metropolitan Police were responsible for London

1) The Metropolitan Police Force was created in 1829, the first of a number of police forces established in England. It was based in Scotland Yard in London, and was responsible for most police activity in the capital. The only area it didn't look after was the very centre of London, which had its own police force — the City of London Police.

2) The force was split into divisions, and each one held responsibility for a particular area of London.

Unlike other British police forces, the Metropolitan Police were answerable to the Home Secretary, who was responsible for law and order in Britain. The Home Secretary also decided who should be appointed as the Commissioner of Police, the highest position in the Metropolitan Police force. This meant that it was important for senior members of the force to work closely with the Home Secretary.

Unfortunately this didn't always happen — see p.82

3) Initially, the role of the police was to prevent crime by 'walking the beat' (see p.78), deterring (putting off) criminals from committing crime and arresting those they saw involved in crime.

4) By the 1870s, more importance was placed on solving crimes. The detective branch of the Metropolitan Police was reorganised into the Criminal Investigation Department (CID) in 1878 (see p.48). Their role was to investigate crimes and find out who had committed them.

The Quality of Police Recruits was Poor

1) Even though working in the police meant a steady job, the general standard of most police recruits was low. Recruit training was basic, with just two weeks of military drill (marching) training and one week of patrol training. Standards of discipline could be poor, e.g. many officers were sacked for drunkenness or for failing to do their duty properly.

Comment and Analysis

The poor quality of recruits made fighting crime harder, and meant local people had less faith that the police could look after them.

2) There were some attempts to improve the quality of the recruits. Sir Edmund Henderson, who became Police Commissioner in 1869, introduced Schoolmaster Sergeants to teach reading and writing to illiterate officers, helping them to do their jobs more thoroughly. Under Henderson, more people were encouraged to apply — some of the strict rules that policemen had to follow were abolished, such as not being allowed to grow a beard or vote. This made police jobs seem more attractive.

3) Under Sir Charles Warren, Police Commissioner from 1886 to 1888, standards for recruits were made tougher. By 1888, recruits had to be aged 21-32, 5 foot 9 inches tall (to look intimidating), and able to read and write well. They were also banned from owning a business or having more than two children so they could focus on the job.

Before this, most recruits were local, working-class men. Their poor health was likely the result of the poverty and poor housing they experienced (see p.72).

4) Ex-soldiers and agricultural workers were also recruited, as they were thought to be stronger, healthier and more used to physical work than city men.

The Public's Attitude to the police was Mixed

1) Not everyone was happy with the police. Some were concerned that they were too much like an army, especially after Warren's reforms. The Metropolitan Police were criticised for reacting too violently in some cases (e.g. during an 1887 protest in Trafalgar Square against the poor treatment of Irish people in Ireland), but for incompetence in others (e.g. for failing to catch the Ripper killer — see p.80 and 82).

2) However, others were more supportive of the police. For example, some people saw the police's firm response to protests as necessary and appreciated the role of the police in upholding the law.

Policing in the Late 19th Century

Try these activities to test your knowledge of the Metropolitan Police and its organisation.

Knowledge and Understanding

The diagram below shows the structure of the Metropolitan Police Force in the late 19th century.

1) Copy and complete the diagram, filling in the details in the boxes on the right about the system of policing in London.

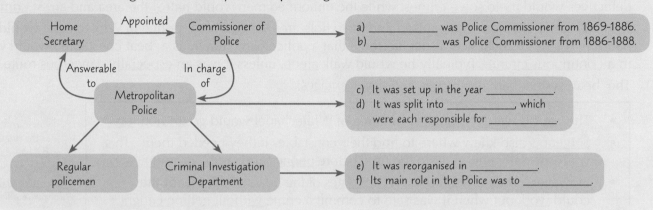

a) _____ was Police Commissioner from 1869-1886.
b) _____ was Police Commissioner from 1886-1888.

c) It was set up in the year _____.
d) It was split into _____, which were each responsible for _____.

e) It was reorganised in _____.
f) Its main role in the Police was to _____.

Source Analysis

The source below is an abridged extract from an article published on 27th October 1888 in *The Western Daily Press*, a local newspaper in southern England. The author discusses comments made by the Police Commissioner, Sir Charles Warren, in defence of the Metropolitan Police.

> ...Sir Charles Warren declares that, whatever the public may think,... the peace and good order of the metropolis* and the prevention of crime depend upon the uniform policemen. The value of the detective branch itself is but a drop in the ocean for all the myriads** of common-place offences which might develop readily into serious crime if not looked after by the uniform police and by citizens. Sir Charles denies that the metropolitan police have been turned into soldiers. He insists, however, that with a force of 14,000 men, the first and most essential point is administration and discipline...

*London   **very large numbers

1) In the boxes below, there are three possible investigations about the Metropolitan Police. Which investigation do you think the source above would be most useful for? Explain your choice.

a) How did constables in the Metropolitan Police feel about the criticisms they faced in the 1880s?

b) What criticisms did Charles Warren's Metropolitan Police face in 1888?

c) How widespread was public disapproval of the Metropolitan Police after 1888?

2) Why do you think the source would be less useful for the other two investigations?

Being a Policeman in London was no easy job...

Avoid making general statements about the usefulness of sources — instead, think about the features of each source that make it useful for the specific investigation you've been given.

Policing Whitechapel

Being a policeman in Whitechapel in the late 1800s wasn't easy — crime was common and hard to tackle.

Whitechapel was looked after by H Division

1) H Division was responsible for policing in Whitechapel. However, because Whitechapel bordered the City of London, the Metropolitan and City of London police forces had to work together in Whitechapel.

2) Like other divisions, H Division had two parts — uniformed police and CID detectives (see p.76). The detectives would try to solve crimes, while the uniformed men would patrol the area and arrest criminals.

3) To make sure policing was organised and the whole area was covered, police in Whitechapel would patrol in 'beats'. A beat was a specific route that a policeman (known as a 'beat constable') would walk in a continuous circuit. Typically he would walk alone, unless it was an especially dangerous route.

4) The 'beat' system had advantages and disadvantages:

> - The patrols were thorough — no area of Whitechapel would go unmonitored.
> - Sergeants also knew where to find their constables if they needed them. This was especially important in the time before phones and radio communication.
> - However, criminals could learn the routes of the beat, which meant they could work out when it was safe to commit a crime without getting caught.

> Some members of the public might have taken reassurance from the regular presence of police officers.

Policing Whitechapel was Tough

Whitechapel's particular features meant that crime was common and difficult to tackle:

- The rookeries (see p.72) were full of winding dark alleys and cramped spaces. There were many places for criminals to hide from the police or attack victims without being seen.
- Many in Whitechapel suffered from alcohol addiction, and drinking increased the chance of being involved in a crime, both as a victim and as a perpetrator.
- Prostitution was common, and prostitutes were often victims of crime, e.g. attacks by their clients.
- Several gangs operated in Whitechapel. They organised illegal gambling, pubs and fights. They were also involved in protection rackets — this was where gangs threatened local businesspeople and shop owners with violence unless they paid money to the gang.
- Violence towards Jews was common, and they could be targets for protection rackets.
- The police had to handle violent demonstrators. Often the protesters were frustrated at poor working conditions. Some were Jewish immigrants from Whitechapel who supported the principles of socialism or anarchism (see p.74) that they had been familiar with in Eastern Europe.
- The local population was often hostile to the police. Many had links to crime themselves, and some disliked how the police treated protesters — particularly if the protests were against government policies that some felt contributed to poverty in Whitechapel.

Whitechapel police didn't have enough Resources

1) The police didn't have the things they needed to tackle crime in Whitechapel. E.g. they didn't have a lot of manpower — there were fewer police per person in London in the late 1800s than there are today.

2) The police also didn't have uniform and equipment which would guarantee them protection:

> They wore helmets in case of attack, and high, reinforced collars which were effective at preventing garotting (strangling using wire or cord). However, they didn't have the benefit of modern protective wear.

> They had a light to shine in dark alleys and a whistle to get attention. But they were only armed with a truncheon (a short baton), whereas criminals might have knives or even guns.

Policing Whitechapel

These activities will help you get to grips with the problems that policemen in Whitechapel faced.

Source Analysis

The source below is an engraving by French artist Gustave Doré showing policemen on night patrol on an unnamed London street in the Whitechapel area. Doré visited various parts of London, often accompanied by policemen, and recorded what he saw in a series of engravings published in 1872.

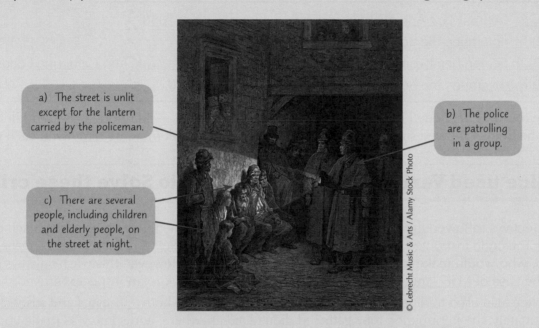

a) The street is unlit except for the lantern carried by the policeman.

b) The police are patrolling in a group.

c) There are several people, including children and elderly people, on the street at night.

© Lebrecht Music & Arts / Alamy Stock Photo

1) Several details from the source have been highlighted in the blue boxes. For each detail, think of a question you could ask to find out more about the challenges of being a policeman in Whitechapel in the 1870s.

2) Give an example of a kind of source that might help you to answer each of the questions you thought of. Explain why it would help you answer the question.

> You can use the examples of types of sources on page 84 to help you.

Knowledge and Understanding

1) Give two reasons why the 'beat' system helped police to fight crime in Whitechapel.

2) Why was the 'beat' system not always an effective way to prevent crime?

3) Copy and complete the mind map below about crime in Whitechapel. For each heading, give as much detail as possible.

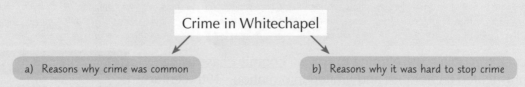

Crime in Whitechapel

a) Reasons why crime was common

b) Reasons why it was hard to stop crime

EXAM TIP

Why did anyone want to be a policeman? It beats me...

When you answer question 2(b) in the exam, you'll start by picking out a detail from the source to follow up on. Make sure your question is clearly linked to the detail you've chosen.

Whitechapel, c.1870-c.1900

Jack the Ripper

The Jack the Ripper case has long been a source of gruesome fascination in Britain. However, the case also highlights developments in police work in the late 1800s — as well as the police's shortcomings at this time.

Jack the Ripper was a Serial Killer in Whitechapel

1) In 1888, a series of brutal murders took place in Whitechapel. All five victims were women, and all were believed to have been prostitutes:

> There were other murders in Whitechapel around this time, some of prostitutes, but only these five are definitely thought to have been performed by the Ripper.

- The first victim, Mary Ann Nichols, was found on 31st August 1888.
- On 8th September, the body of Annie Chapman was found.
- On 30th September, two more victims were found — Elizabeth Stride and Catherine Eddowes.
- On 9th November, the body of Mary Jane Kelly was discovered.

2) All of the murders happened in the street, except Mary Jane Kelly's — her body was found in her house. Most of the bodies showed signs of mutilation, which seemed to get more extreme with each murder.

The police used Various Techniques to try to Solve these crimes

1) The detectives followed the Police Code to decide how to act when they came across each murder scene. The code instructed officers to keep members of the public away until a police inspector arrived, who would make a detailed observation of the scene. However, this wasn't always done — in the case of Mary Ann Nichols, the body was taken away before an inspector arrived.

2) The police also used traditional interview techniques to speak to both witnesses and suspects. Unfortunately, the information they gathered didn't lead anywhere, and some was made up. The police didn't want to offer rewards for information as this encouraged the falsification of information.

3) Autopsies, which involved opening up the body to see what had happened to it and how the victim had died, were already an established technique in murder investigations. All five bodies in the Ripper case were autopsied. The information from these autopsies, particularly the nature of some of the mutilations, led the police to assume certain things about the murderer — especially that he was left-handed, and that he was a butcher or someone with knowledge of anatomy.

4) The police also made sketches of some of the crime scenes, but police sketches at the time were usually drawn in an unrealistic style, and so didn't give the detectives much reliable information.

New Detective Techniques were tried

1) The police used a number of new methods to try and catch the Ripper:

> They took photos during the investigation to record their findings — pictures were taken of Mary Jane Kelly's body and of the room where she was killed, which showed clearly what had happened to her. Previously, the Metropolitan Police had mainly used photos to identify murder victims, often away from the crime scene. In this case, however, they worked closely with the City of London Police, who used photography more frequently.

> The police tried to build up a criminal profile of the killer, bringing together information they had received about him. They thought they were looking for a left-handed, middle-aged man, who was unemployed but with some money, and who wore long coats. This didn't narrow things down very much, as there were many men like this in Whitechapel.

2) However, the police were trying to solve a complex case using unsophisticated techniques and limited information. 19th-century police didn't have the advantages of modern technology like CCTV, or the ability to identify DNA. Keeping mugshots of known criminals didn't become regular practice until the 1890s, and fingerprinting was not used until the early twentieth century.

3) Despite advances made in their techniques during the course of the investigation, the Ripper detectives never caught the killer.

Comment and Analysis

Many of the techniques used in the Ripper case form the basis of modern detective work — taking photographs, conducting interviews, doing autopsies etc. The Ripper detectives, however, were only just beginning to use some of these techniques, and proper procedure wasn't always followed.

Whitechapel, c.1870-c.1900

Jack the Ripper

Use these activities to improve your knowledge of the different techniques used by the police in Whitechapel.

Source Analysis

The source to the right is one of around 80,000 notices printed by the Metropolitan Police after the murders of Elizabeth Stride and Catherine Eddowes on the 30th September 1888. The notices were distributed to houses and tenement buildings around Whitechapel when the police visited local residents to investigate the murders.

1) Imagine you are using the source above for an investigation into the techniques used by the police to investigate the Ripper murders.

   Explain how each of the following features of Source A affects its usefulness for your investigation:

   a) Author   b) Date   c) Purpose   d) Content

POLICE NOTICE.

TO THE OCCUPIER.

On the mornings of Friday, 31st August, Saturday 8th, and Sunday, 30th September, 1888, Women were murdered in or near Whitechapel, supposed by some one residing in the immediate neighbourhood. Should you know of any person to whom suspicion is attached, you are earnestly requested to communicate at once with the nearest Police Station.

Metropolitan Police Office,
30th September, 1888.

Printed by M'Corquodale & Co. Limited, "The Armoury," Southwark.

Notice issued by the Metropolitan Police regarding Jack the Ripper, 30 September 1888 (engraving), English School, (19th century) / Private Collection / Look and Learn / Peter Jackson Collection / Bridgeman Images

Knowledge and Understanding

1) Copy and complete the timeline below, adding in any details you know about the five murders thought to have been carried out by Jack the Ripper, including the names of his victims.

31st August 1888   30th September 1888

8th September 1888   9th November 1888

2) Copy and complete the table below by filling in the limitations or problems with each of these techniques used by the police to investigate the Ripper murders in 1888.

Technique	Limitations or problems
a) **Making a detailed observation of the scene**	
b) **Interviewing witnesses and suspects**	
c) **Drawing sketches of the crime scenes**	

3) What information about the killer did the police believe they had worked out using autopsies?
4) How was the use of photos by the police changing around the time of the Ripper murders?

EXAM TIP

The true identity of Jack the Ripper is still a mystery...

For question 2(a) in the exam, you'll have two different sources to write about. Remember that you should write about each one separately — you don't need to compare them.

Jack the Ripper

The investigation into the Ripper murders was <u>hindered</u> by <u>conflicts</u> between <u>police leaders</u>. The killings also produced a huge amount of <u>public and media interest</u>, but some of it was <u>unhelpful</u> for the investigators.

Cooperation was needed on the Ripper case

1) The Ripper detectives <u>worked closely</u> with <u>other police groups</u>. <u>Extra police</u> were brought in from <u>other divisions</u> to increase <u>manpower</u>, in the hope of catching the Ripper <u>in the act</u>, and to <u>keep the public calm</u>. <u>Experts</u> from the <u>central police detective force</u> at <u>Scotland Yard</u> also <u>helped</u> with the investigation.

2) <u>Cooperation</u> between the different people involved in the Ripper case <u>wasn't always smooth</u>:

<u>Charles Warren</u>, the <u>police commissioner</u> at the time of the Ripper murders, <u>clashed</u> with the <u>Home Secretary Henry Matthews</u>. Warren eventually <u>resigned</u> before the last murder. These <u>arguments</u> made decision-making <u>more difficult</u>, and made the police look <u>disorganised</u>.

After <u>Catherine Eddowes</u> died, some <u>anti-Jewish graffiti</u> was discovered above a bloodied piece of <u>her apron</u>. The <u>City of London</u> Police wanted to <u>photograph</u> the graffiti, but <u>Charles Warren</u> ordered it to be <u>washed off</u> — he feared an <u>anti-Jewish riot</u>, as many people, probably due to <u>prejudice</u> (see p.74), believed the Ripper was <u>Jewish</u>. Warren was <u>criticised</u> for his decision, and had to <u>explain</u> it to the <u>Home Office</u>. This shows that <u>cooperation</u> between the various groups and individuals involved with the case could be <u>complicated</u>.

The Media was Very Interested in the murders

1) The Ripper killings sparked a lot of <u>public interest</u>, and <u>newspapers</u> and <u>magazines</u> published <u>many articles and cartoons</u> on the topic.

2) Many of the claims made in these pieces were purely <u>speculative</u> — jumping to <u>assumptions</u> about <u>who</u> Jack the Ripper was without having any <u>basis in fact</u>.

3) Writers also <u>blamed</u> or <u>mocked</u> the police for not solving the murders. This <u>decreased morale</u> among the police.

© Mary Evans Picture Library

Comment and Analysis

The public and media interest in the murders reflected both the <u>fear</u> and <u>thrill</u> the deaths inspired. The <u>gory details</u> of the deaths, reported by the newspapers, further <u>fuelled</u> this <u>frenzy</u>.

The <u>cover</u> of an <u>1888 publication</u> shows a policeman discovering the body of <u>Mary Kelly</u> in her room. The <u>prominent position</u> given to depictions of the Ripper murders in <u>newspapers</u> and <u>magazines</u> shows how <u>captivated</u> the Victorian public were by the case.

- The high level of <u>media attention</u> made the police's job <u>harder</u>. Many media reports were <u>exaggerated</u> and included <u>unproven claims</u> (e.g. that the killer was <u>foreign</u>). This <u>confused</u> the public's <u>understanding</u> of the murders.

- The police were <u>flooded</u> with <u>false evidence</u>, often motivated by <u>personal vendettas</u>, such as people blaming a neighbour they didn't like.

- The police also had to spend time <u>fending off criticism</u> about the investigation.

<u>Jack the Ripper</u> himself seemed to <u>thrive</u> off this public attention. The press published a number of <u>letters</u> signed from the Ripper, <u>teasing</u> and <u>mocking</u> the police. Many of these are believed to have been <u>fakes</u>, but a few are thought to have <u>really</u> been from the Ripper.

At the time, the police <u>weren't keen</u> on the media — they didn't use the media to <u>appeal for information</u> as they might today. This might have <u>made matters worse</u>, as it encouraged journalists to seek out <u>unreliable witnesses</u> rather than speaking to the police <u>directly</u>.

The Whitechapel Vigilance Committee made things Harder

1) <u>Frustrated</u> that the police hadn't caught the Ripper, a group of local people set up the <u>Whitechapel Vigilance Committee</u>. They <u>patrolled</u> the streets to <u>look for</u> the Ripper and <u>protect</u> the community, and offered their <u>own reward</u> for information. They also hired <u>two private detectives</u> to look into the case.

2) The Committee ended up creating <u>more problems</u> for the police. Much of the evidence they collected was <u>made up</u> — the police spent time <u>looking into</u> some of these leads only to find out they <u>weren't true</u>.

Comment and Analysis

The formation of the Whitechapel Vigilance Committee shows how <u>desperate</u> local people were. However, the time the police <u>wasted</u> following up on <u>false leads</u> could have been spent on finding the <u>real perpetrator</u>.

Whitechapel, c.1870-c.1900

Jack the Ripper

The activities on this page focus on the factors that made it harder for the police to catch Jack the Ripper.

Knowledge and Understanding

1) Give two reasons why conflict between Charles Warren and the Home Office made it harder for the police to investigate the Ripper murders.

2) Copy and complete the diagram below about the media's role in the Ripper murders by explaining how each factor made it harder for the police to investigate the murders.

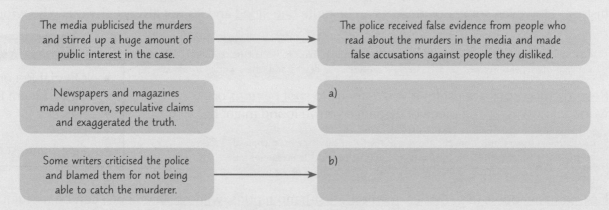

The media publicised the murders and stirred up a huge amount of public interest in the case.	The police received false evidence from people who read about the murders in the media and made false accusations against people they disliked.
Newspapers and magazines made unproven, speculative claims and exaggerated the truth.	a)
Some writers criticised the police and blamed them for not being able to catch the murderer.	b)

3) Explain what the Whitechapel Vigilance Committee was, then describe its role in Whitechapel during the investigation into the Ripper murders in 1888.

Source Analysis

The source below is an extract from an article published in the national newspaper *The London Times* on the 10th November 1888. The article is about the murder of Mary Jane Kelly, whose body was discovered in a lodging house the previous day.

Although the article calls Mary Jane Kelly the seventh victim of Jack the Ripper, it is now commonly accepted that she was the fifth and final victim (see p.80).

> During the early hours of yesterday morning another murder of a most revolting and fiendish character took place in Spitalfields. This is the seventh which has occurred in this immediate neighbourhood, and the character of the mutilations leaves very little doubt that the murderer in this instance is the same person who has committed the previous ones, with which the public are fully acquainted.

1) Imagine you are using the source above for an investigation into how the media portrayed the Ripper murders to the public. Copy and complete the mind map below, explaining why the source is useful for the investigation and why its usefulness might be limited.

Remember to write about the author, date, purpose and content of the source.

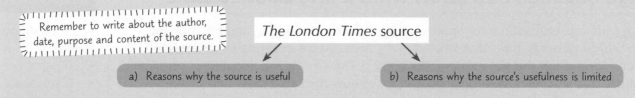

The London Times source

a) Reasons why the source is useful

b) Reasons why the source's usefulness is limited

The media made things harder for the police...

Make sure you use your own knowledge when analysing sources — this will help you to spot factual inaccuracies and to judge the source's usefulness based on the wider context.

Whitechapel, c.1870-c.1900

Types of Sources

When you're writing about the usefulness of sources, it's a good idea to think about what that source can and can't tell you. Some types of sources will give you information that other types of sources don't.

Different Types of Document have different Uses

> Documents are written sources that contain information or evidence.

1) Documents like official records or government reports are useful if you're looking for statistics or factual information about your site and the people who used it.

2) There's often a date attached to official documents too, so you can tell exactly when the source was written. This is useful if you're looking for evidence that's linked to a particular time in your site's history. However, some documents can be quite one-sided and it's not always obvious who wrote them.

> Documentary sources for Whitechapel include housing records, employment records, census returns, social surveys (e.g. Charles Booth's survey on poverty), council records, workhouse records, records of criminal trials, police records, coroners' reports on suspicious deaths, and letters written by officials.

Documents
- Official Records
- Government Reports
- Surveys
- Letters
- First-hand Accounts

3) Record collections are useful if you're trying to spot patterns or work out how typical a piece of evidence you've found might be.

> E.g. Criminal trial records from the archives of the Old Bailey (the main criminal court in the UK) contain the names, ages and charges against the person on trial. These records are useful for understanding which types of crime were common.

4) First-hand accounts (e.g. diaries, memoirs, first-hand reports, witness statements) can be useful for finding out about one person's personal experience of a particular event or site. They often reveal details about a historic site that more official sources might not mention. For example, a diary entry can give a better understanding of what it actually felt like to live through a particular event.

5) When you're using a first-hand account, it's important to look at its provenance (where it's from).

> A personal account written as events were happening might be more accurate than the memoirs of a police officer written years later, as it's easy to forget details, or to focus on some more than others.

> First-hand accounts might be less useful than official documents if you want to find out specific facts. This is because they tend to focus more on personal experience than on technical details.

Newspaper Articles and Letters can reflect Public Opinion

1) Newspaper articles can be useful for analysing public opinion about your site. However, many factors can influence the usefulness of these articles. For example, some articles just told readers what they wanted to hear. This makes them less useful for finding out accurate information about a site, but these articles can still reveal a lot about the attitudes of both the journalist who wrote them and their readers.

2) Opinion letters were published in local and national newspapers during the late 19th century. These letters are useful for showing what people thought about a site. However, they can be less useful for understanding what a site was really like, because they only show one person's opinion and they might have been published because of the author's sensational views.

> To boost their sales, journalists would sometimes use sensationalism. This means exaggerating the facts or focusing on scandalous details to grab a reader's attention.

Image Sources can Show what a site Looked Like

1) Maps are a useful source for looking at how a site was laid out and for showing the buildings or facilities that existed in the area. Maps covering large areas are useful for putting the site into a wider context. Maps of a specific part or physical feature of a site can give a detailed picture of how the site looked and worked.

2) Photographs give a snapshot of a site at a particular time, but every photograph is taken by a photographer who chooses what to focus on and what to leave out.

3) Illustrations show one artist's view, which may be biased towards their own opinion. When you're analysing an image to decide how useful it is, use your own knowledge to decide whether it's giving a typical or accurate picture.

Image Sources
- Photographs
- Maps
- Illustrations
- Cartoons

> Punch cartoons can highlight real issues, but the images are often exaggerated to make them more comical.

Whitechapel, c.1870-c.1900

Types of Sources

Try these activities to help you analyse different types of sources for Whitechapel in the late 19th century.

Source Analysis

1) Copy and complete the table below by listing examples of each type of source and then explaining their strengths and weaknesses. Use your own knowledge, as well as the information on page 84.

Type of source	Examples	Strengths	Weaknesses
a) Documents			
b) Newspaper articles			
c) Image sources			

Source A below is an extract from a letter published in *The Daily Telegraph* on 21st September 1888. The writer, who doesn't reveal their name, describes the conditions on Thrawl Street, where Jack the Ripper's first victim, Mary Nichols, was living before she was murdered.

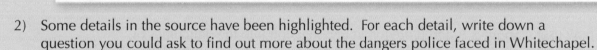

Source A
...the population is of such a class that <u>robberies and scenes of violence are of common occurrence</u>. It is a risk for any respectable person to venture down the turning even in the open day. Thieves, loose women, and bad characters abound, and, although the police are not subject, perhaps, to quite <u>the same dangers as they were a few years ago</u>, there is still reason to believe that <u>a constable will avoid, as far as he can, this part of his beat</u>, unless accompanied by a brother officer.

a)
b)
c)

2) Some details in the source have been highlighted. For each detail, write down a question you could ask to find out more about the dangers police faced in Whitechapel.

3) Give an example of a kind of source that might help you to answer each of the questions you have written. Explain how the source would help you to answer the question.

Source B is an extract from an article called 'An Autumn Evening in Whitechapel'. It was published in an American literary magazine called *Littell's Living Age* on the 3rd November 1888 at the height of the Ripper murders.

Imagine you are using Source B for an investigation into why crime was common in Whitechapel in the late 19th century.

4) How does the purpose of the source affect its usefulness for this investigation?

5) How does the date of the source affect its usefulness for this investigation?

Source B
Turn down this side street out of the main Whitechapel Road. It may be well to tuck out of view any bit of jewellery that may be glittering about... Now round the corner into another still gloomier passage, for there are no shops here to speak of. This is the notorious Wentworth Street. The police used to make a point of going through this only in couples, and possibly may do so still when they go there at all.

Some sources are more useful for putting on chips...

Different types of source are better for answering certain questions. Think about what a source was originally designed to do or say — this'll help you decide how useful it is for your question.

EXAM TIP

Worked Exam-Style Questions

Take a look at these worked answers for some advice on analysing sources about Whitechapel in your exam.

Source A

I have already said something of the extent to which the thieves at large help those who come under the strong arm of the law; and the fact of a man's being "wanted" is a sure passport to the aid of his friends. In Ireland, a couple of years ago, a regular business of getting food and lodging for nothing was established by a class of loafers who went round to the small farmers and represented themselves as being hunted down by the police. They were, of course, enthusiastically welcomed, and it was not until they had carried the game rather too far that it was discovered that they had never done anything to bring them within the pale of the law [...] It is probable that a pseudo-thief would be entertained in the same way in Whitechapel...

Abridged extract from an article entitled 'A Night in Whitechapel', published in 1872 in The Morning Post, *a London newspaper mainly aimed at the upper classes.*

Source B

A cartoon published in the satirical magazine Punch *on 13th October 1888. The caption reads: 'First member of "Criminal Class." "Fine body o' men, the per-leece!" Second ditto. "Uncommon fine!—it's lucky for hus as there's [such] a bloomin' few o[f] 'em!!!"'*

Explain how useful Sources A and B are for an investigation into the difficulties of policing Whitechapel? Use both sources, as well as your own knowledge.   [8 marks]

> **Make it clear which source you're talking about.**

> **Use evidence from the source to support the points that you've made.**

> **Consider whether the information in the source is based on reliable evidence.**

Source A is partly useful for studying the difficulties of policing Whitechapel because it implies that criminals would be 'enthusiastically welcomed' in Whitechapel as the author feels they are in Ireland. Although the author's view of Whitechapel is based on prejudiced ideas about Ireland, Whitechapel was known in the late 1800s for a high rate of crime and hostility to police. This supports the suggestion in the source that criminals were able to evade the police in Whitechapel, and that police efforts to capture criminals might be hindered by the actions of local people.

However, the usefulness of Source A is limited, because it is not clear whether the author actually visited Whitechapel before writing the article. The journalist states that it is 'probable' that Whitechapel residents would protect those who were pretending to be thieves, which suggests that their comments are based on guesswork rather than on the testimony of Whitechapel residents or police. The article's title, 'A Night in Whitechapel', suggests that its purpose was to give the newspaper's readers, many of whom were likely to be upper class people who did not live in Whitechapel, an exciting account of life in Whitechapel. It is therefore

> **Show you know about the wider context and explain what this suggests about how useful the source is.**

> **Ask yourself about the source, e.g. who made it, why and who for.**

Worked Exam-Style Questions

possible that the journalist is exaggerating the level of crime in Whitechapel to make their account more sensational. This makes the source useful for understanding the beliefs held by the journalist and their readers about the difficulties Whitechapel police faced, but it does not necessarily show the realities of policing Whitechapel.

Remember to say how __useful__ you think each source is for __answering the question__.

Remember to write about __both sources__.

Source B is quite useful for studying the difficulties of policing Whitechapel because it suggests that Whitechapel did not have enough police and that criminals thought this was 'lucky' because it was easy to get away with committing crime. This shows that there were concerns about whether there were enough policemen to effectively prevent crime in Whitechapel. As a cartoon in the satirical magazine *Punch*, the message of Source B could be exaggerated to entertain readers.

Think about the __individual source__ and not just __where it's from__.

Consider the __images__ in __visual sources__ as well as any __captions__.

However, the cartoon accurately reflects the narrow, dark streets and alleys that were common in Whitechapel's rookeries, and highlights how easy it was for criminals to hide from the police and commit crimes unseen in this environment, which suggests that it was designed to show the real difficulties of policing Whitechapel.

However, the source was published in October 1888 after Jack the Ripper had murdered four prostitutes, so the concerns it expresses might reflect an especially heightened fear about violent crime in Whitechapel. The police were facing extra difficulties in late 1888 due to needing to catch the Ripper and protect the public, so the suggestion that police numbers were too low may only relate to this specific time. This makes the source less useful for investigating the difficulties facing the police before 1888. The source also does not give the perspective of the police or data on police numbers. Therefore it is useful for highlighting the difficulties that the public believed the police were facing in 1888, but it cannot be used to indicate whether Whitechapel was truly suffering from a shortage of police at this time.

Think about __when__ the sources were created, and how that affects their __usefulness__.

You can also think about what the sources __don't include__.

Explain how you could further investigate Source B to learn more about the difficulties of policing Whitechapel. [4 marks]

Detail from Source B to investigate: The suggestion that there were low numbers of police ('such a bloomin' few') in Whitechapel in 1888.

Make sure your detail is __directly from__ the source.

Ask a question that is __linked__ to the detail you've chosen.

Question you would ask: Were there fewer police in Whitechapel in 1888 than in previous years?

The type of source you might use: Police records that show the number of beat constables in Whitechapel's H Division in 1888 and the years before 1888.

Explain how the source would help you __find out the answer__ to the question.

The type of source you would use should be __quite specific__.

How this could help answer the question: It would reveal whether Whitechapel had a notably low number of beat constables in 1888 compared to previous years.

Whitechapel, c.1870–c.1900

Exam-Style Questions

Here are some exam-style questions for the Historic Environment part of your exam for you to get stuck into.

Exam-Style Questions

1) Give a description of two features of the local population in Whitechapel.   [4 marks]

2) Explain how useful Sources A and B are for an investigation into the issues caused by the media reporting of the Whitechapel 'Ripper' murders? Use both sources, as well as your own knowledge.   [8 marks]

3) Explain how you could further investigate Source A to learn more about the issues caused by the media reporting of the Whitechapel 'Ripper' murders.

   You should give:
   • the detail of Source A that you would investigate
   • the question you would ask
   • what sort of source you might use
   • how the source could help you to answer your question.   [4 marks]

Source A

A British cartoon published on the 20th October 1888 in the satirical magazine *Punch*. The cartoon criticises media reporting of police activity during the 'Ripper' investigation. The caption reads: 'Is Detection a Failure? In the interests of the Gutter Gazette and of the Criminal Classes, the Sensational Interviewer dogs the Detective's footsteps, and throws the strong light of publicity on his work. Under these circumstances, it is not surprising that Detection should prove a failure.'

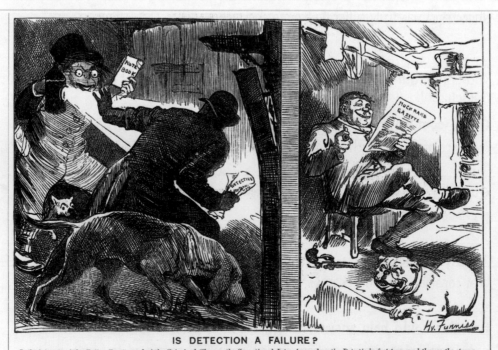

IS DETECTION A FAILURE?

In the interests of the Gutter Gazette and of the Criminal Classes, the Sensational Interviewer dogs the Detective's footsteps, and throws the strong light of publicity on his work. Under these circumstances, it is not surprising that Detection should prove a failure.

© duncan1890/ DigitalVision Vectors/ Getty Images

Whitechapel, c.1870-c.1900

Exam-Style Questions

Source B

A letter sent to Percy Lindley in 1888 by Sir Charles Warren, who became Metropolitan Police Commissioner in March 1886 and resigned from the post in November 1888. Lindley was a breeder of bloodhounds who had written to *The Times* (a national newspaper) to express his support for the idea of using bloodhounds to track Jack the Ripper.

Percy Lindley

York Hill

Loughton

Sir,

I have seen your letter in the Times on subject of bloodhounds and perhaps you could answer a question I have put to many without satisfactory reply.

Supposing a hound to be brought up at once to a corpse after a murder how is he to know what are the tracks or which is the scent of the murderer or how is he to know that you want the particular track tracked.

If the murderer left a portion of his clothing behind and some of his blood I can understand a dog following up or if you could show him a particular spot where he had been standing even but on a London pavement where people have been walking all the evening there may be scores of scents almost as keen as those of the murderer.

This seems to me to be the initial difficulty and I should be glad if you could give me a solution to it.

Truly yours,

C.W. [Charles Warren]

Would a hound follow up a person on whose hands was the blood of a murdered person if he is shown the blood on the ground. I scarcely think he could.

Answers

Marking the Activities

We've included sample answers for all the activities. When you're marking your work, remember that our answers are just a guide — a lot of the activities ask you to give your own opinion, so there isn't always a 'correct answer'.

Marking the Exam-Style Questions

For each exam-style question, we've covered some key points that your answer could include. Our answers are just examples though — answers very different to ours could also get top marks.

Most exam questions in history are level marked. This means the examiner puts your answer into one of several levels. Then they award marks based on how well your answer matches the description for that level.

To reach a higher level, you'll need to give a 'more sophisticated' answer. Exactly what 'sophisticated' means will depend on the type of question, but, generally speaking, a more sophisticated answer could include more detail, more background knowledge or make a more complex judgement.

Start by choosing which level your answer falls into. If different parts of your answer match different level descriptions, then pick the level description that best matches your answer as a whole. A good way to do this is to start at 'Level 1' and go up to the next level each time your answer meets all the conditions of a level. Next, choose a mark. If your answer completely matches the level description, or parts of it match the level above, give yourself a high mark within the range of the level. If your answer mostly matches the level description, but some parts of it only just match, give yourself a mark in the middle of the range. Award yourself a lower mark within the range if your answer only just meets the conditions for that level or if parts of your answer only match the level below.

On this page, you can find the level descriptions for questions in the Thematic Study section of the exam. The level description for the Historic Environment section can be found on page 117.

Level descriptions:

4-mark questions:

Level 1 1-2 marks	The answer gives a simple description of one similarity/difference between features in the two periods. Some knowledge and understanding of the periods is shown.
Level 2 3-4 marks	The answer explains one similarity/difference between features in the two periods. Detailed knowledge and understanding is used to support the explanation.

12-mark questions:

Level 1 1-3 marks	Limited knowledge and understanding of the periods is shown. The answer gives a simple explanation of change/continuity. Ideas are generally unconnected and don't follow a logical order.
Level 2 4-6 marks	Some relevant knowledge and understanding of the periods is shown. The answer contains a basic analysis of reasons for change/continuity. An attempt has been made to organise ideas in a logical way.
Level 3 7-9 marks	A good level of knowledge and understanding of the periods is shown. The answer explores multiple reasons for change/continuity. It identifies some relevant connections between different points, and ideas are generally organised logically.
Level 4 10-12 marks	**Answers can't be awarded Level 4 if they only discuss the information suggested in the question.** Knowledge and understanding of the period is precise and detailed. The answer considers a range of reasons for change/continuity and analyses each one. All ideas are organised logically and connections between different points are identified to create a developed analysis of the topic.

16-mark questions:

Level 1 1-4 marks	The answer shows limited knowledge and understanding of the period. It gives a simple explanation of one or more factors relating to the topic. Ideas aren't organised with an overall argument in mind. There is no clear conclusion.
Level 2 5-8 marks	The answer shows some knowledge and understanding of the period. There is some analysis of how different factors relate to the topic. Ideas are organised with an overall argument in mind, but the conclusion isn't well supported by the answer.
Level 3 9-12 marks	The answer shows a good level of knowledge and understanding of the period, which is relevant to the question. It analyses how several different factors relate to the topic. Most ideas are organised to develop a clear argument and a well-supported conclusion.
Level 4 13-16 marks	**Answers can't be awarded Level 4 if they only discuss the information suggested in the question.** The answer shows an excellent level of relevant knowledge and understanding of the period. It analyses in detail how a range of factors relate to the topic. All ideas are well organised to develop a clear argument and a well-supported conclusion.

Answers

Crime and Punishment in Medieval England, c.1000-c.1500

Page 7 — Anglo-Saxon Crime and Punishment

Knowledge and Understanding

1 a) Stopping people from committing further crimes.
   b) Making criminals pay for their crimes.
   c) A punishment that physically harms the criminal.
   d) When someone is killed as a punishment for a crime.

2 a) • Kings issued their own law codes which stated what counted as a crime during their reign and how serious the punishments should be for these crimes.
      • The Church had its own laws against moral crimes like blasphemy.
   b) Crimes against the person punished by Anglo-Saxon kings included violent robbery, murder and rape.
   c) Crimes against property included arson and theft.
   d) Crimes against authority included breaking the king's peace, harbouring criminals and treason.
   e) • Execution by hanging or beheading was used for serious crimes.
      • Mutilation (e.g. removal of body parts) could be used for lesser crimes.
      • Flogging (whipping) was mainly used to punish slaves.
      • Those who had committed minor offences could have their legs locked in the stocks or their head and arms locked in the pillory.

3 Mutilation left scars and permanent damage which were visible to others. This was meant to deter people from committing similar crimes, because they would be afraid of suffering the same punishment.

4 • The wergild was a set fine that criminals had to pay to their victim in cases of deliberate injury, or to the victim's family in cases of murder. The amount to be paid was based on the king's laws, and depended on the location of the injury as well as the social status of the victim.
   • Paying wergild allowed the victim or the victim's family to get retribution for the crime committed against them without the need for further bloodshed. This prevented lengthy blood feuds developing between families.

Thinking Historically

1 a) • Only the most serious crimes could result in execution.
      • Lesser crimes were punished depending on how serious they were thought to be. Crimes that weren't serious enough to result in execution were still punished severely by mutilation, but minor offences like drunkenness received a less severe punishment, such as being locked in the stocks or the pillory.
   b) • The wergild depended partly on social status — for example the wergild amount due for killing a nobleman was higher than the amount due for killing a serf.
      • Most crimes committed by slaves were punished by flogging.

2 You can choose either option, as long as you explain your answer. For example:
   I agree that the severity of the punishment usually depended on the severity of the crime, because Anglo-Saxon punishments aimed to make the criminal pay appropriately for the crime they committed. Other factors sometimes contributed to the severity of punishments. For example, the social status of the victim influenced the amount of wergild that was due. However, most of the time, the severity of the punishment was linked directly to the severity of the crime. There was a clear ranking of crimes, with punishments ranging from execution for serious crimes like murder, to being locked in the stocks for a minor offence like drunkenness, meaning the harshest punishments were usually used for more serious crimes.

Page 9 — Anglo-Saxon Law Enforcement

Knowledge and Understanding

1 a) A method of law enforcement where local people shouted or made a loud noise to alert everyone in the area to a crime so the criminal could be pursued.
   b) A group of local men summoned by the shire-reeve to help him catch criminals.
   c) A small group of men over the age of twelve who were responsible for bringing to court any member of the group who had been accused of a crime.

2 The king:
   • He created laws that everyone in the kingdom had to follow.
   • He was responsible for keeping the peace in his kingdom.
   Earls:
   • They were responsible for enforcing the law within their earldom, but they had to rely on local representatives to govern the shires and hundreds in their earldom.
   • They were in charge of shire courts.
   Shire-reeves:
   • They governed shires on behalf of the king and the earl.
   • They attended shire courts to collect fines and make sure the law was being followed.
   • They ran shire courts if the earl was unable to attend.
   • They could call a 'posse comitatus' to catch criminals.
   Reeves:
   • They enforced the law within hundreds.
   • They ran the hundred courts in their area.
   • They brought criminals to justice on the king's behalf.

3 a) Collective responsibility is the idea that everyone in a group or community is responsible for making sure that the law is upheld.
   b) There was no police force in Anglo-Saxon England, so communities had to police themselves.
   c) The Anglo-Saxon system for catching criminals and bringing them to court was based on collective responsibility. The tithing system, in which each member of a tithing was responsible for the behaviour of everyone else in the group, relied on collective responsibility to work. Any member of a tithing who was accused of a crime had to be brought to court, or the whole tithing would be fined. In addition, ordinary people had a duty to stop what they were doing and help search for accused criminals when the hue and cry was raised.
   d) Collective responsibility was an effective method of law enforcement because Anglo-Saxon communities were very small and everyone lived, worked and worshipped together. This meant that people were likely to know who had committed a crime and where to find them.

Thinking Historically

1 You can choose either opinion for each statement, as long as you explain your answer. For example:
   a) I mostly disagree with this statement, because the king wasn't directly involved in making sure that his laws were being obeyed. Although the king was responsible for maintaining law and order in his kingdom, local representatives enforced his laws on his behalf, meaning his role in day-to-day law enforcement was minimal.

Answers

b) I mostly disagree with this statement, because shire-reeves played a key role in local law enforcement by representing the king and the earl at a shire level. They were responsible for collecting fines and making sure that the law was being followed across the shire by attending shire courts. Although they weren't as involved as reeves in the day-to-day affairs of the local community, they still played an active role in law enforcement because they were responsible for organising the 'posse comitatus' to help catch criminals.

c) I mostly agree with this statement, because the tithing played the most active role in local law enforcement by taking on collective responsibility for upholding the law. Although the king's representatives were responsible for actually enforcing the law in court, tithings were responsible for bringing criminals to court in the first place. As tithings were made up of local people who were in a good position to know who had committed a crime and where they could be found, their role in capturing criminals was essential.

Page 11 — Trials in Anglo-Saxon England
Knowledge and Understanding

1 a) Oaths played an essential role in deciding whether an accused person was guilty or innocent in Anglo-Saxon trials. In trials by compurgation, the accused person had to swear an oath of innocence, as well as gathering compurgators who also had to swear an oath that the accused was telling the truth about their innocence.

b) The verdict of an Anglo-Saxon trial could depend on the reputation of the accused in the local community. If the accused had a reputation for being trustworthy, people would be more prepared to be compurgators for them. Someone with a bad reputation would struggle to find enough people willing to swear that they were innocent.

2 • When the court was unable to reach a verdict.
  • When the accused couldn't find enough compurgators.

3 a) • Usually used for men.
  • The accused had to fast and pray for three days before the trial, then they had to plunge their arm into boiling water. This trial usually took place in a church.
  • If the wound was healing well after three days, the accused was innocent. If it wasn't, they were guilty.

b) • Usually used for men.
  • The accused had to fast and pray for three days before the trial, then they were tied up and thrown into a pool of cold water that had been blessed by a priest.
  • If the accused sank, the water (and God) was thought to have accepted them, so they were declared innocent. If they floated, the water was seen to have rejected them, meaning they were considered guilty.

c) • Usually used for women.
  • The accused had to fast and pray for three days before the trial, then they had to walk a short distance while carrying a red-hot iron bar, usually in a church.
  • If the wound was healing well after three days, the accused was innocent. If it wasn't, they were guilty.

Thinking Historically

1 a) Evidence for — Churchmen played a key role in trials by ordeal, as trial by boiling water and trial by hot iron usually took place in a church, and trial by cold water required the involvement of a priest to bless the water. Trial by ordeal was an essential part of the Anglo-Saxon system of determining whether someone was guilty or innocent.

Evidence against — Trial by ordeal was often a last resort. Churchmen only played a big role in trials when trial by compurgation had failed to determine a person's guilt. Local people and representatives of the king played the most important role in these trials by compurgation.

b) Evidence for — The outcome of a trial by ordeal was based on chance. For example, a person who was tried by boiling water was seen as guilty if their wound wasn't healing well after three days, which was an outcome that could occur whether a person was guilty or not. Evidence against — Trials by compurgation relied on local people stating whether or not a crime had taken place. Anglo-Saxon communities were small and tight-knit, so local people would often be in a good position to know what had happened.

2 You can choose either option, as long as you explain your answer. For example:
Local people played a more important role in law enforcement because they were involved in many more aspects of local law enforcement than the Church was. Although the Church had an important influence over law enforcement through Church courts and through its role in trials by ordeal, local people had a more direct influence on law enforcement in general. Local people heard court cases and decided the verdict, as well as acting as witnesses and compurgators. Local people could actively prove someone's innocence through compurgation, or cause the accused to go through a trial by ordeal by refusing to swear oaths to their honesty. Local people also had an active role in law enforcement in the community through systems like tithings and the hue and cry.

Page 13 — Norman Crime and Punishment
Knowledge and Understanding

1 William I kept most of the Anglo-Saxon laws because he wanted to be seen as the rightful successor of the Anglo-Saxon king, Edward the Confessor, who died in 1066.

2 The murdrum fine was a fine that Anglo-Saxons had to pay if a Norman was murdered in their area and the killer wasn't caught. William I introduced this fine to try to protect Normans from being attacked by Anglo-Saxons.

3 a) Forest law was introduced to give the king and certain nobles exclusive hunting rights in parts of the country.

b) Before forest law, people in England could hunt and forage for food in most parts of the country, but forest law made this illegal. This led to the creation of the crime of poaching, which involved hunting on someone else's land without their permission.

c) Punishments for poaching included being blinded, having fingers removed so you were unable to draw a bow, or even being executed.

4 A social crime is an offence that is not thought to be wrong by most people. In Norman England, most people didn't think poaching should be a crime because they thought the laws against it were unfair.

Thinking Historically

1 a) William's army marched to the north of England, where they killed hundreds of people, burned crops and homes, and destroyed livestock. This became known as 'the harrying of the north'.

b) William wanted to prevent any more rebellions in the north by removing the rebels' support and supplies. He also wanted to punish the rebels harshly to deter other people from rebelling against his rule.

Answers

c) William gradually replaced the remaining Anglo-Saxon nobles with Norman nobles.

d) Nobles were responsible for enforcing the law in their area, so this meant the law was now enforced by Normans, who were more likely to support William as king.

2 a) William I's laws had a significant impact on Anglo-Saxon communities because they affected the daily lives of ordinary people. Forest law led to entire villages being uprooted to make way for the king's hunting grounds in the New Forest, and it took away their hunting rights, making it harder for them to feed their families. The murdrum fine meant that whole communities might have to pay a fine if a Norman was murdered.

b) William I kept most existing Anglo-Saxon laws in place when he became king, meaning many Anglo-Saxons were able to live as they had before. Although he also introduced new laws, these only had a significant impact on certain Anglo-Saxon communities. For example, the changes made under forest law only directly affected those living in or near royal forest areas, and the murdrum fine only affected communities if a murder took place.

c) Overall, I agree that William I's laws had a significant impact on Anglo-Saxon communities. The changes that resulted from forest law took away the basic rights of some Anglo-Saxons. While William's laws might only have affected certain communities or groups in society, their impact on these communities was significant, as people were forced to change their way of life.

Page 15 — Norman Crime and Punishment
Knowledge and Understanding
1 • Execution was still used to punish serious crimes.
• Corporal punishments, such as whipping and mutilation, were still used to punish less serious crimes.
2 a) How it stayed the same:
• Criminals were still fined for committing certain crimes.
How it changed:
• Fines for causing injury or death went to the king instead of to the victim or their family.
b) How it stayed the same:
• Trial by ordeal was still used to settle cases where swearing oaths and producing witnesses had failed to determine guilt.
How it changed:
• A new ordeal of trial by combat was introduced.
• Anglo-Saxons were able to use trial by combat or trial by hot iron to defend themselves if they were accused of crimes like murder and robbery by a Norman.

Thinking Historically
1 • Local nobles, shire-reeves and reeves were still in charge of local law enforcement.
• The hue and cry and tithings were still used to catch criminals.
• Shire and hundred courts were still used to try criminals.
2 a) • Castles were built in strategic locations to help maintain law and order and prevent unrest.
b) • Earls became less powerful and lost control over the shire courts.
• Sheriffs became more powerful, acting as the king's main representative in the shires and taking over shire courts. Some sheriffs were given control of castles.
c) • Normans took overall control of law enforcement, as Anglo-Saxon nobles had been replaced with Normans by 1100.

3 You can choose either opinion, as long as you explain your answer. For example:
The Norman Conquest was not very significant in changing crime and punishment in England, because most of the laws, punishments and methods of law enforcement under the Normans were the same as they had been during the Anglo-Saxon period. Although the new crime of poaching was created and a new trial by ordeal was introduced, most Anglo-Saxon laws were still in place, and both capital and corporal punishments continued to be used in much the same way as they had been in Anglo-Saxon England. Similarly, while the Anglo-Saxon nobles were replaced by Norman nobles, most methods of law enforcement, such as tithings and the hue and cry, were still in place. This suggests that law enforcement continued to rely on the idea of collective responsibility.

Page 17 — The Later Middle Ages
Knowledge and Understanding
1 a) Royal judges were appointed from 1166 to travel the country and hear the most serious cases in each area. This meant that the law was enforced more consistently.
b) Coroners were appointed from 1194 to investigate suspicious deaths and ensure that fines owed by criminals reached the king.
c) Keepers of the Peace were appointed from 1195 to uphold the law in areas where there was disorder. In 1327, Keepers of the Peace were appointed in all areas.
d) Justices of the Peace developed out of the role of Keeper of the Peace. They upheld the law by imprisoning criminals, judging cases and hanging the guilty.
2 These new roles were introduced to help enforce the law in local communities. The growth of towns meant that it was no longer the case that everyone knew each other, so it became harder for communities to police themselves.
3 a) • According to the 1351 Treason Act, high treason was defined as any attempt to overthrow or harm the king or the royal family.
• Those found guilty of high treason could be hanged, drawn and quartered from 1351. In reality, many traitors were beheaded or hanged instead.
b) • Heresy was defined as speaking out against the Church or its beliefs.
• People who committed heresy, known as heretics, could be arrested and tried in Church courts from 1382. From 1401, heretics who refused to give up their beliefs could be burned at the stake.

Thinking Historically
1 The increase in the number of royal officials in the later Middle Ages made the system of law enforcement more centralised. This meant that the king had greater control over law enforcement through his officials, who acted locally on his behalf. This allowed the king to make sure that his laws were being enforced consistently across the country. It also meant that the role of local people in law enforcement was reduced because local people had less responsibility for policing themselves.
2 a) Examples of continuity:
• Some actions, such as murder, arson and theft, were recognised as crimes throughout this period. Treason also remained a serious crime throughout the period.
Examples of change:
• The new crime of poaching was created by the Normans when forest law was introduced after the Norman Conquest.

- The Statute of Labourers in 1351 made it a crime to demand higher wages from your lord, move away from your lord's land to seek higher wages, or to work for more than a set maximum wage.
- High treason was redefined by the 1351 Treason Act as any attempt to overthrow or harm the king or his family.
- Heresy became a crime from the late 14th century onwards.

b) Examples of continuity:
- Throughout the period, local people played a role in enforcing the law in their communities through systems like the hue and cry.
- The king continued to rely on royal representatives such as sheriffs to enforce his laws.

Examples of change:
- Trial by combat, a new form of trial by ordeal, was introduced by the Normans to determine whether someone was guilty.
- More responsibility for local law enforcement was shifted to sheriffs under the Normans as earls lost some of their power.
- The court system was reorganised in 1166 and royal judges were appointed to travel across the country to hear the most serious cases in each area.
- The role of coroner was created in 1194. Coroners looked into suspicious deaths and made sure that fines owed to the king were paid.
- Keepers of the Peace were appointed from 1195 to uphold the law in areas where there was disorder. In 1327, they were appointed in all areas and later became known as Justices of the Peace. Justices of the Peace could imprison criminals, judge cases and hang guilty people.
- New local law enforcement roles such as parish constable and watchman were created to help communities police themselves.
- The king had greater control over how his laws were enforced by the later Middle Ages, because the increase in the number of royal officials meant the system of law enforcement became more centralised.

c) Examples of continuity:
- The aims of punishment were mainly deterrence and retribution throughout the period.
- Execution was used throughout the medieval period to punish serious crimes.
- Fines continued to be used as a punishment.

Examples of change:
- The Normans replaced the Anglo-Saxon wergild with a new system of fines. Fines owed for deliberate injury or murder were now paid to the king rather than to the victim or their family.
- The Normans introduced the murdrum fine to punish whole communities if a Norman was murdered and the killer wasn't caught.
- A new punishment of hanging, drawing and quartering was introduced for high treason.
- After 1401, heretics could be punished by being burned at the stake.

3 You can answer either way, as long as you explain your answer. For example:
- Overall, there was more change than continuity in crime and punishment during the medieval period. Although the local community still played a role in enforcing the law, the system of law enforcement became increasingly centralised. This meant that

the king had more control over how his laws were enforced through royal officials like Justices of the Peace. Although many offences, such as murder, were recognised as crimes throughout this period, some new crimes were created, such as poaching and heresy. There were also important changes to the way that crimes were punished. The aims of punishment were still generally deterrence and retribution. However, the introduction of the punishments of hanging, drawing and quartering for high treason in 1351, and burning at the stake for heresy in 1401, reflected how harsh punishment was increasingly being used to protect the authority of the king and the Church.

Page 19 — Case Study: The Influence of the Church

Knowledge and Understanding

1 Moral crimes were actions that went against the social or religious rules of the time.

2 Church courts tried different kinds of crimes than secular courts did. They generally tried moral crimes such as blasphemy. The punishments handed out by Church courts were often more lenient than those given in secular courts, so that criminals had a chance to repent. For example, the Church didn't execute criminals. Church courts also had the power to excommunicate criminals (exclude them from the religious community).

3 Benefit of Clergy was a privilege that applied to clergymen who were accused of crimes. It allowed them to avoid the death penalty by standing trial in the more lenient Church courts. In order to claim Benefit of Clergy, criminals had to prove they were a clergyman by reading out a passage from the Bible. Criminals who weren't actually clergymen could take advantage of this by learning the passage so they could recite it to avoid execution.

4 a) Sanctuary was the right of accused criminals to seek shelter inside a church so they couldn't be arrested for their crime.

b) To claim sanctuary, the accused had to enter a church, ring a particular bell or door knocker, or in some cases step into an area marked by sanctuary posts.

c) Sanctuary usually only lasted 40 days. In some cases, the criminal had to pay a fine or give up their property to be granted sanctuary.

Thinking Historically

1
- The Church used its influence to make heresy illegal in the late 14th century.
- The Church was responsible for trying and punishing moral crimes.
- The Church influenced the punishment of crime through its own courts. Clergymen were able to claim Benefit of Clergy so they could be tried in a Church court, which didn't use the death penalty. Others benefited from this too because they could claim Benefit of Clergy by reciting a specific passage of the Bible, even if they weren't clergymen.
- The Church hindered the capture of criminals by offering sanctuary to fugitives.
- The Pope stopped clergymen from taking part in trials by ordeal in 1215. Without priests to oversee them, trials by ordeal became far less common.

2 You can answer either way, as long as you explain your answer. For example:
Overall, the Church had the biggest influence on crime and punishment in the later Middle Ages because it

Answers

played a big role in determining how crimes were tried and punished in this period. Although the king defined secular crimes and enforced them through royal courts and officials, the Church had an important influence on the enforcement of both secular and religious laws. The Church had its own courts to try moral crimes, such as blasphemy, while religious privileges meant that they could also influence how secular crimes were punished. For example, the Church could help criminals to temporarily escape the king's justice by offering sanctuary, and Benefit of Clergy gave criminals a chance to avoid the death penalty. The Church also caused a decline in the use of trials by ordeal when the Pope decided to prevent priests from taking part in them in 1215.

Page 21 — Exam-Style Questions

1 This question is level marked. You should look at the level descriptions on page 90 to help you mark your answer. Here are some points your answer may include:
- Capital punishment was used in both periods. During the Anglo-Saxon period, offences such as arson and theft could be punished with hanging or beheading. In the later Middle Ages, crimes such as treason and heresy were punished with execution.
- Crimes against authority were punished harshly in both periods. Treason (plotting against the king) was punishable by death in both the Anglo-Saxon period and the later Middle Ages.
- Some punishments were intended to be visible deterrents in both periods. Corporal punishments used in Anglo-Saxon England, such as whipping and mutilation, left scars and permanent damage which people could see, deterring others from committing the same crimes. In the later Middle Ages, high treason was punishable by being hung, drawn and quartered. The pieces of the traitors were displayed in public so others could see them, deterring others from committing treason.

2 This question is level marked. You should look at the level descriptions on page 90 to help you mark your answer. Here are some points your answer may include:
- Poaching became a crime after the Norman Conquest because William I wanted to secure hunting rights for himself and Norman nobles. After the Conquest, William introduced forest law, which made large areas of England royal forest, areas of land where only the king and certain nobles were allowed to hunt. Before this, ordinary people could hunt and gather food in most parts of England, but the new law meant that it was a crime to hunt in the royal forest without permission.
- Killing a Norman became a crime in the 11th century because William I wanted to protect Norman settlers. After the Conquest, Normans were a minority in England so they were vulnerable to violent attacks from Anglo-Saxons. This led William to introduce the murdrum fine to protect Normans from violence. If a Norman was killed and the murderer wasn't caught, then local Anglo-Saxons had to pay this fine.
- New labour laws were created in the mid-14th century because of changes in society caused by the Black Death. Around a third of the population was killed by the Black Death, resulting in a shortage of labour. The nobles who owned land didn't want their surviving workers asking for higher wages. This led to the passing of the Statute of Labourers, which made it a crime for workers to demand higher wages from their lord, seek higher wages elsewhere or work for more than a set maximum wage.
- Heresy became a crime in the late 14th century because churchmen felt threatened by those who were speaking out against the Church. The Church's fears led to laws being passed against heresy, meaning it could be tried as a crime in Church courts from 1382.

3 This question is level marked. You should look at the level descriptions on page 90 to help you mark your answer. Here are some points your answer may include:
- The king played an important role in law enforcement in Anglo-Saxon England because had overall responsibility for keeping the peace in his kingdom. He was responsible for deciding what acts were crimes and appointed representatives, such as earls and shire-reeves, to enforce his laws.
- The King often took an active role in law enforcement in the medieval period. For example, King William I responded directly to a major Anglo-Saxon rebellion in the north of England by carrying out 'the harrying of the north'. His army killed hundreds of people, burned crops and homes, and destroyed livestock. This suggests that the king was actively involved in punishing criminals as well as setting down the law.
- In the later Middle Ages, the king had even more control over law enforcement as new royal officials were introduced to enforce the law, creating a more centralised system. For example, from 1195, the king appointed Keepers of the Peace to uphold the law in areas where there was disorder. By 1327, Keepers of the Peace were appointed in all areas, and later became known as Justices of the Peace. This meant that the king had more control over law enforcement across the whole country.
- Despite the growing influence of the king in the medieval period, local communities continued to play an important role in law enforcement. In Anglo-Saxon England, everyone in the local community had to participate in the hue and cry to help catch a suspected criminal. This system was still in use in the later Middle Ages, and local people also played a key role in enforcing the law by working as constables and night watchmen in this period. Therefore, local people often played a more important role than the king because they had a much more active role in catching criminals.
- Although the king was in charge of keeping the peace in this period, his representatives played a more important role in actually enforcing the law. For example, in the Anglo-Saxon and Norman periods, sheriffs were often responsible for running local shire courts, collecting fines and making sure the law was being followed. In the later Middle Ages, royal officials, such as coroners, Keepers of the Peace, and then Justices of the Peace, had an increasing influence over law enforcement. For example, Justices of the Peace were responsible for imprisoning criminals, judging cases and hanging the guilty. As a result, royal representatives were much more involved in the actual process of law enforcement than the king was.
- Although the king was responsible for making most laws in this period, the Church played a more important role in law enforcement than the king overall, because it had a great influence on both moral and secular law. The Church ran its own courts, which tried people for moral crimes, demonstrating that the Church had ultimate power over the enforcement of moral law in the medieval period. However, the Church also had a great influence over secular law. For example, the Church could protect

Answers

clergymen from being tried in an ordinary court by offering them Benefit of Clergy. In addition, the Church offered criminals sanctuary, giving them the opportunity to temporarily escape punishment from the king's representatives.

Crime and Punishment in Early Modern England, c.1500-c.1700

Page 23 — Religious Changes

Knowledge and Understanding

1 The Act of Supremacy made Henry VIII the head of the English Church, but he still held Catholic beliefs. This meant that people who wanted England to be more Protestant were still committing heresy because they were speaking out against the Catholic head of the English Church.

2 A movement where England broke away from the Catholic Church and became more Protestant. It was part of a wider movement in Europe in the 16th century.

3 a) The 1549 Act of Uniformity made it compulsory for people to use the Book of Common Prayer, a book of Protestant Church services, for worship. People who refused to do so could be fined or imprisoned.

   b) After Mary became queen, the Book of Common Prayer was banned.

   c) The 1559 Act of Uniformity made Protestantism the official faith of England and introduced fines for people who refused to attend Protestant church services.

4 There were threats to Elizabeth's rule that made her become less tolerant of Catholics in the 1570s. The Pope encouraged Catholics to remove her from the throne after he excommunicated her in 1570, and there were also many Catholics who wanted Elizabeth's Catholic cousin Mary, Queen of Scots, to take the throne. Later in Elizabeth's reign there were Catholic plots against her.

Thinking Historically

1 The 1534 Act of Supremacy meant that heresy could also be considered treason. The Act made Henry VIII head of the English Church, giving him religious authority in England. This meant that those who committed heresy by refusing to accept Henry's authority over the Church were also committing treason because they were going against the authority of the king.

2 a) • Opposition to the changes introduced by the 1549 Act of Uniformity was considered to be heresy. This meant that Catholics who opposed the move towards Protestantism were committing heresy.
   • Punishment of heresy was quite moderate. Heresy laws introduced in Henry's reign were repealed, and only two people were executed for heresy under Edward.

   b) • Continuing to practise Protestantism was considered to be heresy.
   • Heresy was punished very severely. Hundreds of Protestant clergymen and ordinary people were executed by being burned at the stake.

   c) • The 1559 Act of Uniformity made Protestantism the official faith of England, which meant that Catholics could now be punished for heresy again.
   • Punishment for heresy was quite moderate, as few Catholics were executed for heresy. However, punishment of Catholics was still harsh, with around 250 being executed for treason during Elizabeth's reign.

3 The definition of heresy changed several times in early modern England because different monarchs had different religious beliefs which caused them to make changes to England's laws. For example, under Edward VI, rejecting Protestant ideas was considered heresy, whereas under Mary I people could be found guilty of heresy if they practised Protestantism. The religion of the monarch affected the definition of heresy because religious authority in England had transferred from the Pope to the monarch. For example, the 1534 Act of Supremacy meant that Henry VIII and his son Edward VI were heads of the English Church during their reigns, while Elizabeth I's 1559 Act of Supremacy made her Supreme Governor of the Church of England.

Page 25 — Social and Economic Developments

Knowledge and Understanding

1 A vagabond was a person who moved from place to place looking for work or begging.

2 • 1531 — Beggars without a licence are punished by whipping and the stocks.
   • 1547 — The 1547 Vagrancy Act is passed. This Act punishes people who choose not to work by forcing them to work as slaves for up to two years.
   • 1549 — The 1547 Vagrancy Act is repealed.
   • 1572 — The Vagabonds Act is passed, stating that vagabonds can have a hole burnt through their ear and repeat offenders can be executed.
   • 1593 — Punishments as part of the 1572 Vagabonds Act are removed.
   • 1597 — The Act for the Relief of the Poor means that relief for those who are too old or ill to work is organised by Overseers of the Poor. Vagabonds are still punished by whipping.

3 a) • Smuggling means moving things in and out of a country illegally.
   • Smuggling was hard to police because there weren't enough officers on the coastline to be effective against smugglers, who often used violence to escape arrest.

   b) • Poaching is the act of illegally hunting on private land.
   • Poaching was hard to police because many people ignored poaching laws.

Thinking Historically

1 a) • The population grew rapidly. Between 1485 and 1603, the population of England doubled to around 4 million.
   • The rising population contributed to food shortages and an increase in food prices. This meant many people couldn't afford food, so they turned to poaching as a way to feed their families.

   b) • Lots of land was fenced off in a process known as enclosure. Many farmers also switched from growing crops to farming sheep.
   • Enclosure fenced off land which people had previously been able to farm to feed themselves and their families. This made it harder for people to grow their own food, so they turned to poaching instead. The farmers' decision to farm sheep meant they required fewer workers which caused people to become unemployed. This led to people becoming vagabonds.

   c) • Monasteries were being closed by Henry VIII from 1536.
   • Monasteries had traditionally fed and sheltered the poorest people. The closing of the monasteries meant poor people had to support themselves in different ways, either by poaching or becoming vagabonds and

Answers

begging. In addition, the closure of the monasteries led some people to commit treason by rebelling against Henry's decision in an uprising called 'The Pilgrimage of Grace'.

2 a) Social and economic changes influenced definitions of crime in the early modern period because they caused an increase in the number of vagabonds, which led the government to introduce the new crime of vagabondage. Poverty levels rose as a result of population growth and rising food prices. Farmers also switched from growing crops to farming sheep. This required fewer workers, so many people became unemployed and fell into poverty. The rising number of poor and unemployed people meant that vagabondage became more of a problem, so the government acted to discourage vagabondage by making it a crime.

   b) Social attitudes influenced definitions of crime in the early modern period because they caused the government to recognise vagabondage as a crime. While some poor people were seen as deserving of help, others were labelled as vagabonds and were seen as a serious threat to society. It was feared that they would encourage riots and rebellions. The government responded to this threat by making vagabondage illegal.

   c) The government had a big influence on the definitions of various crimes in the early modern period. Several monarchs, from Henry VIII to Elizabeth I, changed how the crime of heresy was defined by introducing new laws that changed the official religion of England, such as Elizabeth I's 1559 Act of Uniformity. Henry VIII's 1534 Act of Supremacy also changed how treason was defined by blurring the lines between treason and heresy. The government also introduced laws that made vagabondage a crime.

3   You can choose any of the factors, as long as you explain your answer. For example:
   • The government had the biggest influence on definitions of crime in the early modern period. While social attitudes and social and economic changes created the conditions that led the government to make vagabondage a crime, it was the government that actually changed the law. The government also played a significant role in the changing definition of heresy during the 16th century. Heresy was redefined several times, depending on the religious views of the monarch in power. These changes were motivated by the monarch's own beliefs, not social attitudes or social and economic changes.

Page 27 — Early Modern Law Enforcement
Knowledge and Understanding
1   A thief-taker was a person paid by the government or victims of a crime to find and capture criminals.
2   • The population of England's towns increased significantly. Many of the people who moved to towns in this period came to look for work. Towns were increasingly home to successful businesses and rich citizens.
   • The larger population meant that it was harder to catch criminals, because it was easier for criminals to go unnoticed and people didn't always know each other. In addition, many of the people who came to towns to find work but were unsuccessful turned to crime in order to survive. The large number of rich people and successful businesses meant there were

more opportunities for crimes like theft and fraud to be committed.

3   • 1512 — Laymen who commit certain crimes such as murder and highway robbery can no longer claim Benefit of Clergy. These offences become 'unclergyable'.
   • 1536 — Clergymen can no longer claim Benefit of Clergy for 'unclergyable' offences.
   • 1540 — The right to seek sanctuary is removed for serious crimes such as murder, arson and rape.
   • 1623 — James I passes a law that abolishes sanctuary for any crime.

Thinking Historically
1   • In both periods, sheriffs were responsible for policing local communities.
   • In both periods, sheriffs were responsible for organising local trials.
   • In both periods, sheriffs could call a 'posse comitatus' to find criminals.

2   • Existing law enforcement officers became less effective — towns continued to grow in the early modern period, making it even more difficult to identify criminals within these communities than in the later Middle Ages.
   • The ineffectiveness of law enforcement officers such as constables and night watchmen led to the development of new law enforcement roles, such as thief-takers.
   • Sheriffs lost some of the powers they'd had in the later Middle Ages because the role of Justices of the Peace grew.
   • By the end of the 16th century, Justices of the Peace no longer tried capital cases as they had done in the later Middle Ages.
   • A small salary was introduced for night watchmen in London in 1663.
   • By the late 17th century, many richer townspeople hired someone else to take their place as the night watchman.

3 a) There was more change in the role of the Church in law enforcement. Due to the growth of royal power in this period, the Church lost some of its power over law enforcement. For example, the growth in the number of 'unclergyable' offences meant that fewer criminals were tried in Church courts, reducing the Church's role in enforcing the law.

   b) There was more change in the role of the government in law enforcement. There was some continuity, because royal officials continued to be responsible for maintaining law and order on the monarch's behalf. However, overall there was more change as royal power over law enforcement grew when Church privileges like sanctuary and Benefit of Clergy were reformed. The government also began to directly fund law enforcement at the end of the early modern period by introducing fixed rewards for thief-takers.

   c) There was more continuity in the role of local communities in law enforcement. Many features of local community policing from the medieval period, such as the hue and cry and 'posse comitatus', remained in the early modern period. Local people still took on roles like constable and night watchman to enforce the law within their community.

Answers

Page 29 — Transportation and the Bloody Code

Knowledge and Understanding

1 Flogging was still used in the early modern period to punish minor offences. For example, beggars could be whipped.

2 Punishments were often carried out in public to deter people from committing crimes. For example, punishments like the stocks and flogging aimed to humiliate and shame criminals so they wouldn't commit more crimes.

3 Transportation was a punishment where criminals were sent to work in English colonies, either for life or for a fixed period of time. It was a way of making a harsh sentence like execution less severe.

4 There was nowhere to transport prisoners to until the 1600s because English settlers only began to establish colonies in North America in 1607.

5 The introduction of the Bloody Code meant that many minor crimes were classed as capital offences. The number of crimes punishable by death increased from fifty in 1688 to several hundred under the Bloody Code. Many of these crimes were minor offences against property.

Thinking Historically

1 The Bloody Code developed because Parliament gained more power in the 17th century. The monarch had the most control over law and order at the start of the 17th century. However, royal power was weakened because of the English Civil War in the 1640s and the introduction of the English Bill of Rights in 1689, which gave Parliament more freedom to pass laws. Many members of Parliament were landowners, so they wanted the law to protect property. This led to Parliament making more crimes against property punishable by death.

2 a) • Public punishments such as the stocks were used for minor crimes to shame criminals in both periods.
   • Corporal punishments such as flogging were used to punish minor crimes in the medieval period and in the early modern period.
   • Execution was used to punish serious crimes in both periods.
   • Criminals guilty of high treason could be hung, drawn and quartered in both periods.
   • Heresy was punishable by being burned at the stake at the end of the medieval period and in the early modern period.
   • Prisons weren't used as a punishment in their own right in either period.
   • Fines were used to punish minor offences in both periods.
   • Punishments focused on deterrence and retribution in both periods.

   b) • Transportation was only introduced in the early modern period.
   • Laymen and clergymen could no longer avoid punishment for serious crimes by the end of the early modern period because Benefit of Clergy was reformed.
   • From the late 17th century, punishment for minor crimes became harsher under the Bloody Code.
   • Hanging, drawing and quartering was used more frequently to punish traitors in the early modern period.

3 You can answer either way, as long as you explain your answer. For example:
   • There was more change in punishment between these two periods. Minor crimes were punished more harshly towards the end of the early modern period as a result of the development of the Bloody Code. This differs from the medieval period when minor crimes were punished using corporal punishments such as whipping and mutilation. While some crimes did keep similar punishments, the Bloody Code marked a significant change by making death the ultimate deterrent for many crimes.

Page 31 — Case Study: The Gunpowder Plotters

Knowledge and Understanding

1 a) A group of Catholics led by Robert Catesby begin to plot against the King. They make a plan to blow up barrels of gunpowder beneath Parliament when James is due to be there on 5th November 1605. They aim to make James's daughter queen and appoint a regent to rule for her, most likely someone who is sympathetic to Catholics.

   b) Lord Monteagle reveals the warning to one of the King's advisors.

   c) Other plotters, including Catesby, are killed in a gun battle.

2 Guy Fawkes was tortured as part of an interrogation. One of the plotters died in prison while awaiting trial, and the other captured plotters, including Guy Fawkes, were hung, drawn and quartered for high treason. Their body parts were sent to various areas of London to be publicly displayed.

3 James I punished the Gunpowder Plotters brutally to establish his authority and deter others from committing treason. England was still unstable because of religious changes in the 16th century caused by the English Reformation, so James I was at risk of other acts of treason by Catholics who were unhappy with how they were being treated.

Thinking Historically

1 a) The government influenced how harsh anti-Catholic laws were. For example, Elizabeth I introduced heavier recusancy fines because she faced the threat of Catholic plots after being excommunicated in 1570. James I also tightened laws against Catholics in 1604 when he saw that people disapproved of his more lenient approach to Catholics. After the Gunpowder Plot failed, the government introduced even harsher anti-Catholic laws.

   b) Although James I was initially pro-Catholic, Catholics were so unpopular with most people in England that public attitudes forced him to change his approach. He reintroduced recusancy fines and tightened laws against Catholics in 1604 when people expressed disapproval of his more tolerant approach to Catholics.

2 • Catholics were banned from voting.
   • Catholics were banned from certain occupations, such as becoming lawyers or army officers.
   • Fines for recusancy were increased again.
   • Catholics had to swear a new oath of loyalty to the monarch.
   • Anti-Catholic attitudes increased, with many people blaming Catholics for crises like the Great Fire of London and plots against the monarch.

Answers

Page 33 — Witchcraft
Knowledge and Understanding

1   In the medieval period, witchcraft was generally tolerated as long as it wasn't used to commit a crime. However, attitudes became less tolerant in the 1400s. A book on witchcraft called 'Malleus Maleficarum' claimed all witches should be treated as heretics and put to death.

2   Church courts did not order the death penalty, so nobody could be executed for witchcraft before the 1540s.

3   • 1542 — Parliament passed England's first Witchcraft Act. Witchcraft became a crime against the king and state, meaning it was tried by the king's judges rather than in Church courts. This meant harsher punishments such as execution could be used.
    • 1547 — The 1542 Witchcraft Act was repealed under Edward VI. Witchcraft was no longer punishable by execution.
    • 1563 — A new Witchcraft Act was passed under Elizabeth I. The Act was similar to the 1542 Act, except execution could only be used if witchcraft had caused someone's death.
    • 1604 — A stricter Witchcraft Act was passed under James I. The death penalty was expanded to anyone found guilty of calling up evil spirits or keeping familiars.

4   The witch craze was a period of panic over witchcraft in the 17th century when hundreds of people were put on trial for witchcraft. Many of those accused were poor, old women, widows or local 'wise women' with healing skills.

Thinking Historically

1   The swimming test worked in a similar way to trial by cold water. Guilt was determined in both trials by tying the accused up and putting them into a pool of water. The accused would be guilty in both cases if they floated, and innocent if they sank. People believed in both cases that if the person floated, it meant that God had rejected them.

2 a) • The printing press meant books like 'Malleus Maleficarum' and 'Demonology' could be printed and distributed to many people. This contributed to an increase in the number of witch trials because these books fuelled the paranoia over witchcraft that led many people to accuse others of the crime.

  b) • James I had strong beliefs that witchcraft was evil. His book 'Demonology' spread these beliefs and caused people to fear witches, leading to an increase in the number of witch trials as more people were accused of witchcraft.
    • The witchcraft laws introduced by monarchs between 1542 and 1604 made it possible for royal judges to try people for witchcraft and pass the death sentence.

  c) • People in local communities began to believe that witches could cause them harm with their magic. This made people scared of witchcraft and encouraged them to accuse people of being witches.
    • People began to believe that their misfortune was caused by the actions of witches in this period. As a result, they looked for a 'witch' to blame when something went wrong for them. This led people to accuse their neighbours of witchcraft, contributing to an increase in the number of witchcraft trials.

Page 35 — Case Study: Hopkins and Witch-hunts
Knowledge and Understanding

1   Matthew Hopkins was a witch finder who operated in south-eastern England in the mid-1640s. He helped to stir up the witch craze by offering to find witches in local communities for a fee, and using the suspicion and ill will of local people to create cases against suspected witches. He organised the trials of around 250 accused witches between 1645 and 1647.

2   Hopkins was criticised by some people who felt he was forcing innocent people to confess to witchcraft so that he could earn his fees. Hopkins justified his methods in his pamphlet, 'The Discovery of Witches', which was partly a response to the accusations against him.

3 a) Hopkins made the accused stand for days at a time or forced them to stay awake.

  b) Hopkins would strip the accused naked and search for a 'Devil's mark', a scar, mole, boil or birthmark from which it was believed a familiar could suck the witch's blood.

4   A Puritan was an extreme Protestant who wanted to make England more Protestant by removing Catholic influences from the Church.

5   There was religious and political instability in England because the religious division created by the English Reformation was continuing to cause tension between Protestants and Catholics. There was also tension between these groups and the Puritans, who had gained lots of political power in England by the 1630s. The Puritans wanted to make England more Protestant and remove Catholic influences from the Church. This period was also marked by political instability, leading to the English Civil War in the 1640s, when the monarchy and Parliament clashed over religion and power in England.

Thinking Historically

1   • Political instability in this period may have encouraged local leaders to use witch trials as a way of imposing some order on their communities, because they felt their authority was threatened.
    • The Civil War meant that many people distrusted those who behaved or thought differently to them. This made people more likely to suspect each other of witchcraft.
    • The breakdown of law and order caused by the Civil War meant that some communities took the law into their own hands. Witch finders like Hopkins were able to take advantage of this situation by encouraging communities to accuse witches.

2   You can choose any of the factors, as long as you explain your answer. For example:
    Political instability was the most significant factor in fuelling the witch craze in the 1640s. Although monarchs played an important role in passing laws that made witchcraft illegal, it was the political instability caused by religious divides and the Civil War that allowed men like Matthew Hopkins to take advantage of people's paranoia and suspicion to organise the trials of hundreds of witches. Political instability created conditions where local people were more suspicious, and the disorder caused by the Civil War meant that communities were able to take the law into their own hands. Therefore, is unlikely that Hopkins would have had such a big influence on the witch craze if it wasn't for the unstable political situation caused by the Civil War.

Answers

Page 37 — Exam-Style Questions

1 This question is level marked. You should look at the level descriptions on page 90 to help you mark your answer. Here are some points your answer may include:
- Constables played a key role in law enforcement in towns in the medieval period and in the early modern period. In the later Middle Ages, parish constables were responsible for upholding the law in their area and leading the hue and cry to capture suspects. During the early modern period, town constables kept the peace in towns, and arrested criminals.
- Night watchmen played a role in law enforcement in towns in both periods. In the later Middle Ages, local citizens served as night watchmen, watching for crime and handing over anyone who committed a crime to the constable the next day. In the early modern period, night watchmen still assisted constables by patrolling the streets at night.
- Local people were involved in law enforcement in towns in both periods. Throughout the medieval period, local people were responsible for joining the hue and cry to catch criminals. They could also be summoned by the shire-reeve to join a 'posse comitatus'. These practices continued in the early modern period, as sheriffs could still call a 'posse comitatus' and local people still had to join in the hue and cry.
- Sheriffs (or shire-reeves) played an important role in managing law enforcement in towns in both periods. In the Anglo-Saxon period, shire-reeves attended local shire courts to collect fines and ensure the law was being followed. In the early modern period, sheriffs were responsible for policing local communities and organising local trials.

2 This question is level marked. You should look at the level descriptions on page 90 to help you mark your answer. Here are some points your answer may include:
- Restrictions were placed on Benefit of Clergy in the 16th century that changed the way some offences could be punished. From 1512, any layman who committed serious crimes like murder or highway robbery could no longer claim Benefit of Clergy. From 1536, clergymen were also unable to claim Benefit of Clergy if they committed an 'unclergyable' offence. This meant that criminals guilty of serious crimes could no longer be protected from the death penalty for certain crimes, because both laymen and clergymen could no longer claim Benefit of Clergy for many offences.
- Witchcraft became punishable by execution due to the actions of the government. In 1542, Parliament passed the Witchcraft Act, which made witchcraft a crime against the king and state. This meant it could be tried by the king's judges rather than in Church courts, making it possible for harsher punishments, such as execution, to be used. In 1604, James I passed another, harsher Witchcraft Act that reflected his personal intolerance of witchcraft. This Act meant that anyone who was found guilty of calling up evil spirits or keeping 'familiars' could be punished by execution.
- Vagabonds faced harsh punishments because they became more of a problem for the government. In the 16th century, social and economic changes created a rise in poverty and unemployment that forced many people to turn to vagabondage to survive. In response to this, the government made vagabondage a crime and passed new laws that introduced harsh punishments

for vagabondage. For example, from 1531, vagabonds could be whipped, while the 1572 Vagabonds Act stated that vagabonds could be executed. This response was a result of fears that vagabonds would encourage riots and rebellions against the government.
- Opportunities for different kinds of punishment were created in the 17th century. English settlers began to establish colonies in North America in 1607. This allowed the government to introduce the new punishment of transportation, where criminals were sent to work on the colonies as an alternative to the harsh punishment of execution.
- Crimes against property were punished more harshly because Parliament gained more power to pass laws after the English Civil War in the 1640s and the 1689 English Bill of Rights. Many Members of Parliament were landowners, so they used their increased power to introduce the Bloody Code, a series of harsh laws that applied the death penalty to minor property crimes.

3 This question is level marked. You should look at the level descriptions on page 90 to help you mark your answer. Here are some points your answer may include:
- In the 14th century, changes in society led to the introduction of new labour laws that created new crimes. From 1348 to 1351, the Black Death killed around a third of the population, meaning workers were in higher demand. Landowners didn't want the surviving workers asking for higher wages, so the Statute of Labourers was passed in 1351. This made it a crime for workers to demand higher wages, move away from their lord's land to seek higher wages elsewhere, or work for more than a set maximum wage.
- Changes in society in the 16th century led to vagabondage becoming a crime. Due to rapid population growth, poor harvests and changes to farming practices, lots of people became unemployed or fell into poverty. This led to an increase in vagabonds, who moved around looking for employment or begging. As a result, the government introduced new laws that made vagabondage a crime.
- The role of the government was more important in changing definitions of crime in Norman England. For example, William I created the new crime of poaching by introducing forest law, which classed large areas of England as 'royal forest' and made it a crime to hunt and forage in these areas without permission. William created this law because he wanted to establish exclusive hunting rights for himself and his nobles, suggesting that the government played a more important role in creating the crime of poaching than changes in society.
- The government played a more important role in defining crimes against authority in this period. In the 16th century, the crimes of heresy and treason were redefined several times, depending on the will of the monarch in power at the time. For example, under Edward VI, heresy was defined as opposition to Protestantism because Edward was a Protestant, whereas under Mary I, who was a Catholic, heresy was defined as opposition to Catholicism.
- The Church also had an impact on changing definitions of crime against authority in the later Middle Ages. The Church used its influence to make heresy illegal from the late 14th century because it felt threatened by heretics. While this change was a result of the Church's fear of heresy in society, it was the actions of the Church and the

Answers

government that actually led to heresy becoming a crime.

- The government had the biggest influence on the definition of witchcraft as a crime in this period. Parliament passed the 1542 Witchcraft Act, which made witchcraft a crime against the king and the state, while James' introduction of a new, stricter Witchcraft Act in 1604 expanded the definition of the crime of witchcraft. This shows that the government was in control of what was considered witchcraft in this period.

Crime and Punishment in Britain, c.1700-c.1900

Page 39 — Poaching, Smuggling and Robbery
Knowledge and Understanding
1 a) The Waltham Black Act was a law created in 1723 that introduced the death penalty for around fifty minor crimes. It made being in a hunting area while carrying hunting equipment and having a blackened face a capital offence.
   b) There had been a rise in organised poaching gangs who worked together to hunt large numbers of animals and sell them. The government introduced the Waltham Black Act to tackle these gangs.
   c) The Act was repealed in 1823 as part of Robert Peel's reforms.
2 They were a well-known smuggling gang who had a reputation for using violent methods. They ran a large-scale smuggling operation in the 1730s and 1740s on the south coast of England.
3 a) • Taxes had been placed on more imported goods, such as tea, in the late 17th century, making smuggling more attractive.
   • Trade with other countries had grown, meaning that there were lots of items produced overseas that people wanted to buy. This meant that smuggled goods, which were cheaper to buy than legally imported goods, were in popular demand.
   • Organised gangs started to carry out smuggling operations on a large scale.
   b) • Smuggling often happened at night in secluded coastal areas, so it was difficult to monitor.
   • Many people supported smugglers because they benefited from their activities, making it harder for the authorities to catch smugglers.
   c) • The government lowered taxes on imported goods like tea, which gave people less incentive to smuggle.
   • The authorities built watchtowers on the south coast to make it easier to spot smugglers.
   • The authorities formed the Coast Guard which made it easier to catch smugglers.
Thinking Historically
1 The Waltham Black Act could be considered a turning point in the punishment of minor crime because it introduced the death penalty for around fifty minor crimes, as well as introducing very harsh punishments for offences related to poaching. This increase in the number of capital offences contributed to the growth of the Bloody Code in the early 18th century, which saw hundreds of crimes made into capital offences. Therefore, the Waltham Black Act played a key role in transforming the way that minor crimes against property were punished in Britain.
2 a) • Growth — The banking system wasn't very developed, so people often travelled with valuables and money, making them profitable targets for highway robbers.

- Decline — There was an increase in the use of banknotes. This made it easier to catch highway robbers because banknotes were easier to trace.
   b) • Growth — Towns were far apart, meaning travellers had to use long roads in remote rural areas where it was easy for robbers to attack. There were more carriages on the roads, which meant that highway robbers had more targets. People started to travel together in stagecoaches a lot more during this period, so highway robbers could steal from several people at once.
   • Decline — Patrols were introduced on major roads, which deterred highwaymen. Roads were also made more secure because of enclosure and the introduction of turnpike gates, where travellers had to pay a toll to pass. This made it more difficult for highway robbers to escape after they had committed a robbery.

Page 41 — Changing Definitions of Crime
Knowledge and Understanding
1 a) The farm workers gather support from other workers and ask them to swear an oath of solidarity and pay a subscription to join the union.
   b) The six union leaders are found guilty and sentenced to seven years' transportation to Australia. This is the maximum sentence possible.
   c) 100,000 people gather in Copenhagen Fields near King's Cross in London to protest against the union leaders' sentence.
   d) In 1836, the government pardons the union leaders and allows them to return home.
2 The authorities responded harshly because they wanted to discourage other workers from setting up their own trade unions. This is because trade unions campaigned for better pay and working conditions for workers. This worried the authorities because the French nobility had been overthrown by the working class in a series of revolutions, and the British authorities thought something similar might happen in Britain if working people gained too much power.
Thinking Historically
1 In the early modern period, people were fearful of witchcraft due to the influence of monarchs such as James I and books such as 'Malleus Maleficarum'. However, by the mid-18th century, there had been developments in scientific understanding which meant that most educated people no longer believed that witchcraft was real. Despite this, many ordinary people continued to believe in witchcraft.
2 You can choose any of the factors, as long as you explain your answer. For example:
   The role of the Royal Society was the most important reason for the change in witchcraft laws. Although the government was responsible for passing the new Witchcraft Act in 1736, the Act was passed because attitudes towards witchcraft had changed. This change probably wouldn't have happened without the influence of the Royal Society. The Royal Society encouraged educated people to think in a more scientific way rather than believing in superstition. This led many people to question whether witchcraft really existed, which was reflected in the 1736 Witchcraft Act's statement that witchcraft was not real.

Answers

3   Similarities:
- In both cases, the authorities used harsh punishment to deter others from committing the same crime. William carried out 'the harrying of the north', which devastated parts of the north, because he wanted to prevent future rebellions. Similarly, the Tolpuddle Martyrs were given the maximum sentence possible so that other workers would be deterred from setting up their own trade unions.

Differences:
- Although the authorities responded harshly in both cases, William's response to the 1069 rebellion was harsher. His army killed hundreds of people and destroyed people's crops, homes and livestock. In contrast, the Tolpuddle Martyrs were given the punishment of transportation.
- William continued to treat Anglo-Saxons harshly after 'the harrying of the north' by taking away their land and giving it to his Norman supporters. However, the authorities in the 19th century pardoned the Tolpuddle Martyrs after large-scale public protests against their treatment.

Page 43 — Changing Views on Punishment
Knowledge and Understanding
1 a) Execution was abolished as a sentence for all but the most serious crimes, such as murder and treason. Previously, execution had been used to punish lots of minor crimes.
   b) Public executions were abolished. After 1868, all executions were carried out behind closed doors.
2
- Public executions were criticised by important individuals such as Charles Dickens for lacking a serious atmosphere.
- There was usually trouble at public executions because there were large crowds of people who often got drunk.
- Public executions caused more crime, as pickpockets and prostitutes regularly attended public executions to target the large crowds.
3
- Some convicts stayed because they weren't allowed to leave Australia.
- Some convicts stayed because they couldn't afford the journey back to England from Australia.
- Some convicts stayed because they wanted to live in Australia. They felt they had more opportunities there than in England.

Thinking Historically
1
- 1718 — A law was passed making transportation an official alternative to the death penalty. This caused an increase in the number of people being punished with transportation.
- 1775/1776 — The American War of Independence began in 1775, and no convicts were sent to America after 1776. This caused a decrease in the number of people being punished by transportation.
- 1787 — The government began transporting convicts to Australia. This caused an increase in the number of people being punished by transportation.
- 1840s — Australian settlers began to complain about convicts being sent there. Some people in Britain questioned the effectiveness of transportation at deterring people from committing crime. The use of prisons had also grown in England, offering an alternative to transportation. These changes caused a decrease in the number of people being punished by transportation.

- 1868 — The last convicts sent to Australia arrived. No criminals were punished by transportation after this point.
2
- Juries were reluctant to convict someone for a minor crime if it meant they would get the death penalty. Juries didn't want to treat petty thieves in the same way as murderers. As a result, some criminals were going unpunished and crime was actually being encouraged.
- There was religious opposition to the Bloody Code. Some religious people claimed that it was against God's law to execute people for minor crimes.
- Prisons and transportation were seen as suitable alternative punishments to the death penalty. This meant that criminals who committed less serious crimes could be given a more lenient sentence, instead of being punished by death.

Page 45 — Prison Reform
Knowledge and Understanding
1   Prisons were mainly used to hold people before a trial or execution.
2   Jailer's fees had to be paid to wardens by prisoners so they could be released from prison. If prisoners couldn't afford the jailer's fee, they would have to remain in prison.
3   Quakers believe that God is present in everyone, so they believe criminals have the ability to change and behave morally. This belief may have led Quakers to encourage others to give prisoners the chance to reform themselves.

Thinking Historically
1 a) Living conditions in prisons were poor and needed to be improved. Prisons were usually dark, dirty and damp, which led to the spread of diseases such as dysentery and typhus. Prisoners also had to pay wardens for food and would share the worst cells with many other inmates if they couldn't pay fees to jailers.
   b) Prisons were increasingly being used as a form of punishment, because the use of transportation had largely ended by the mid-1850s, and the Bloody Code was abolished in 1861. This created a rise in prisoners, encouraging the government to make changes to prisons.
   c) Although some people believed prisons should be harsh and unpleasant to deter criminals, those on the other side of the debate felt that prisons should try to rehabilitate inmates. This interest in rehabilitation encouraged people to try to reform prisons.
2   John Howard:
- He toured the country studying prisoners' poor living conditions. His findings prompted Parliament to pass laws to improve prison conditions.
- His work led to an Act that ended the use of jailer's fees.
- His work led to an Act that required prisons to provide a safe and hygienic environment for prisoners and to give them access to medical care.

Elizabeth Fry:
- She worked to improve living conditions at Newgate Prison.
- She campaigned successfully for the separation of male and female inmates, the introduction of female jailers and the introduction of paid jobs for prisoners to earn money.
3   You can answer either way, as long as you explain your answer. For example:
John Howard had the most significant impact on prison reform. His work began the process of improving prison conditions, and it encouraged Parliament to pass two Acts

in 1774 that helped to improve the safety of prisons and created better living conditions for prisoners. This set new standards for prisons, and laid the foundation for further reforms like those of Elizabeth Fry in the 1800s.

Page 47 — Case Study: Pentonville Prison
Knowledge and Understanding
1 Joshua Jebb designed Pentonville Prison which was a model of the 'separate system'. Jebb's prison was intended to provide better living conditions than many existing prisons in Britain.

2 It declared that the 'separate system' should be used in prisons. The 'separate system' meant that prisoners were isolated from each other, which was supposed to allow them to be rehabilitated at the same time as punishing them and deterring them from committing more crimes. The Act led to many new prisons, such as Pentonville, being built to make it easier for the 'separate system' to be used.

3 a) Both — Separate cells gave prisoners their own space which they hadn't always had in old prisons. They also helped the use of the 'separate system' by isolating prisoners from each other.
b) Living conditions — Cells were more comfortable to live in than in earlier prisons.
c) 'Separate system' — This kept inmates away from more hardened criminals and gave them time to reflect on their crimes.

4 • Some people, including Elizabeth Fry, felt that the system didn't give inmates a real chance to change their ways.
• The system led to psychological problems and suicides among inmates.
• Some people felt the system wasn't harsh enough because it wasn't deterring prisoners from committing more crimes.
• Some people believed that most prisoners belonged to a 'criminal class'. This led them to criticise the 'separate system' because they thought there was no point in using a system that aimed to reform criminals if criminals were incapable of changing their ways.

Thinking Historically
1 a) Evidence for — Pentonville inmates had their own cells so that they had time to reflect on their crimes, giving them the opportunity to reform themselves.
Evidence against — Prisoners' cells were cramped, with just enough space for one person, making them uncomfortable to live in. This was meant to punish prisoners and deter them from committing more crimes.
b) Evidence for — After 1865, life became harsher in prisons as prisoners had to work for several hours a day, eat dull food and sleep on uncomfortable beds. Prisoners were also banned from speaking to each other. Before the Act, there had been more of a focus on rehabilitating prisoners through the 'separate system' rather than just punishing them.
Evidence against — Prisoners were punished harshly before the 1865 Prisons Act. Solitary confinement was already in place as part of the 'separate system' and conditions inside prisons were tough. For example, prisoners lived in cramped cells and had to wear masks when they left their cells so they couldn't see other prisoners.

c) Evidence for — The government introduced Acts, such as the two in 1774 and the 1865 Prisons Act, that controlled how prisons were reformed.
Evidence against — The work of individuals such as John Howard and Elizabeth Fry encouraged the government to make changes to how prisons were run.

2 You can answer either way, as long as you explain your answer. For example:
a) • The main purpose of Pentonville prison was to both reform and deter criminals. Although Pentonville was designed with the 'separate system' in mind, which isolated prisoners from one another so they could reflect on their crimes, conditions in the prison were still deliberately tough so that criminals would be deterred from committing more crimes. For example, cells only provided just enough space for one person. As Pentonville was designed around a regime based on the dual aims of reform and deterrence, Pentonville's purpose of deterrence can be seen as just as important as its aim to reform criminals.
b) • The Prisons Act of 1865 was a turning point in the process of prison reform because the Act officially changed the purpose of prisons so that there was a movement away from helping prisoners. Before 1865, prison reform had focused on improving conditions in prisons and then on trying to introduce ways of rehabilitating prisoners. The 1865 Act changed this, so that prison reform became focused on making conditions in prisons worse to punish criminals.
c) • Individuals played a more significant role than the government in prison reform in this period. The work of John Howard encouraged the government to make big changes to prisons, such as introducing two Acts in 1774 that improved prison conditions. Elizabeth Fry was also very influential in reforming prisons. She campaigned successfully for the separation of male and female inmates, the introduction of female jailers and the introduction of paid jobs for prisoners. The role of the government was only important because individuals persuaded them to take action.

Page 49 — The Development of Police Forces
Knowledge and Understanding
1 Urbanisation is a process where an urban population increases because many people move from the countryside to cities.

2 • 1749 — The Fielding brothers establish the Bow Street Runners, a group of men who investigate crime and try to catch criminals. They earn money by charging fees, for example when a criminal they catch is convicted.
• 1785 — The government starts to pay the Bow Street Runners for their services.
• 1829 — Home Secretary Robert Peel sets up the Metropolitan Police Force.
• 1842 — The Metropolitan Police sets up a detective department to solve crimes.
• 1856 — The Police Act is passed. This makes it compulsory for all areas across the country to have a police force.
• 1878 — The detective department of the Metropolitan Police becomes the Criminal Investigation Department (CID).

Answers

Thinking Historically

1 a) This made it easier for people to commit crimes and get away without being recognised because not everyone knew each other.

   b) There were more opportunities for theft because those who had profited from the Industrial Revolution had more money and property which criminals could steal, such as merchandise from warehouses.

   c) Many orphans and people experiencing poor living conditions committed crime to earn money and improve their lives.

2 Similarities:
   - Both groups were paid to find and capture criminals.
   - Both groups earned money by charging victims for their services, and both also received money from the government.

   Differences:
   - The Bow Street Runners patrolled the streets, whereas thief-takers in the early modern period were hired to catch specific criminals.
   - Thief-takers in the early modern period worked separately, whereas the members of the Bow Street Runners were part of an organised group.
   - Unlike thief-takers, the Bow Street Runners played an important role in improving national policing. They published a national newsletter that included descriptions of wanted criminals.
   - Thief-takers in the early modern period earned money from the government from fixed rewards after the 1690s, whereas the Bow Street Runners were paid.

3 a) The Metropolitan Police Force were a centralised and structured organisation that employed professional policemen, whereas night watchmen were ordinary people who had to take it in turns to police the streets at night.

   b) The Bow Street Runners were set up and run by London legal officials, whereas the Metropolitan Police Force was government-controlled. The Bow Street Runners were a smaller organisation than the Metropolitan Police Force, and didn't have different departments such as the Metropolitan Police Force's detective department. The Bow Street Runners focused on investigating crime and catching criminals, whereas the Metropolitan Police Force aimed to oversee law and order in London and deter criminals, as well as to investigate crime.

Page 51 — Case Study: Robert Peel

Knowledge and Understanding

1 He was the person in the government who was in charge of law and order.

2 They both believed that prisons should aim to reform prisoners.

3
   - The force aimed to gain the public's trust so people would follow the law voluntarily.
   - Policemen would only use force when it was necessary.
   - The police would be impartial and wouldn't be prejudiced against any groups in society.
   - The force would be judged as effective if there was a lack of crime.

4
   - Some people were worried that a police force would limit their freedom like the strict police force in France had done to the French population.
   - There were concerns about the cost of creating a force.
   - Some people were worried about the risks to privacy.
   - Some people were worried that the police would be like an army.

- Some felt that policing should continue to be conducted locally rather than being government-controlled.
- The force didn't seem very effective at first because the first Metropolitan Police officers were poorly-trained and didn't always act morally.
- The media exaggerated the negative qualities of the new police officers, making the force seem laughable.

Thinking Historically

1 In 1823, Robert Peel introduced the Gaols Act, which ensured that the same standards were applied to prisons across Britain. The Act introduced changes that aimed to help reform prisoners, for example letting chaplains visit them. The Gaols Act also paid jailers a salary so prisoners didn't have to pay jailer's fees to get out of prison, and banned the use of iron restraints on prisoners. Peel also implemented some of Fry's ideas, such as separating male and female prisoners and using female jailers.

2 a) Robert Peel had a more significant impact because his actions led to changes in policing across Britain. He was responsible for setting up the Metropolitan Police, which was the first government-controlled police force. The influence of the Metropolitan Police was far-reaching. Its success led to other police forces being set up across Britain when the 1856 Police Act made a police force compulsory in all areas, and the principles Peel introduced are still used by police forces today. While the Fielding brothers set up the Bow Street Runners, which helped to improve national policing, this was a small organisation that had a more limited impact than the Metropolitan Police.

   b) The Fielding brothers had a greater impact on the development of policing because they set up the Bow Street Runners, who played a key role in improving national policing. The Bow Street Runners introduced methods of policing that had not existed before, such as the use of a national newsletter to better co-ordinate national policing. While the Metropolitan Police had a significant impact on policing, the Bow Street Runners may have paved the way for this organisation to be created by proving that a centrally-controlled police organisation could be effective.

   c) Overall, Robert Peel had a more significant impact on the development of policing because his actions had an effect across the whole country, and his model of policing is still in use today. Although the Fielding brothers may have inspired the development of centrally-organised police forces by setting up the Bow Street Runners, Peel's decision to create the Metropolitan Police was not only a result of the success of the Bow Street Runners. Peel was also concerned about the number of different police organisations that were being used and the use of the army to maintain order.

Pages 52 and 53 — Exam-Style Questions

1 This question is level marked. You should look at the level descriptions on page 90 to help you mark your answer. Here are some points your answer may include:
   - Poaching was punished harshly in both periods. After the Norman Conquest, forest law meant that poachers could be blinded, have their fingers removed or be executed. In 1723, the Waltham Black Act made it a capital crime to be in a hunting area while carrying hunting equipment and having a blackened face.
   - In both periods, poaching was a social crime because many people didn't see it as a serious offence. In

Norman England, people felt that the laws against poaching were unfair because people who had previously been able to live off the land could now be executed for trying to feed their families. Similarly, in the 18th century, ordinary people felt the punishments for poaching introduced by the Waltham Black Act were excessive compared to the offence.

- Certain wealthy individuals were exempt from poaching laws in both periods. Under Norman forest law the king and certain nobles were allowed to hunt in the royal forest. In the 18th century, wealthy landowners were still allowed to hunt wherever they wanted.

2 This question is level marked. You should look at the level descriptions on page 90 to help you mark your answer. Here are some points your answer may include:

- An increase in taxes and the growth of overseas trade led to smuggling becoming more common. Increased taxes encouraged people to import goods illegally so they could avoid paying these taxes. An increase in demand for items that came from other countries, such as tea and tobacco, also contributed to the growth of smuggling because it encouraged smuggling gangs to smuggle these goods to take advantage of popular demand.
- Smuggling decreased in the late 18th century because taxes on imported goods went down and there were improvements in the policing of smuggling. As imported goods became more affordable, people had less incentive to buy goods from smugglers, reducing the demand for smuggled goods. The authorities built watchtowers on the south coast and created a Coast Guard in the 1820s, which made it easier to catch smugglers.
- Highway robbery became more common in the 18th century because there were more opportunities for theft on roads. People often travelled long distances between towns on remote rural roads, so they were an easy target for highway robbers. Many of these people carried large sums of money around with them because the banking system wasn't very developed at this time. There was also an increase in people travelling together in groups by stagecoach. This attracted highway robbers because they could steal from several people at once.
- In the 1830s, there was a decrease in the crime of highway robbery as a result of several factors. The use of patrols on major roads discouraged highway robbers, while an increase in the use of banknotes meant that money was easier to trace if it was stolen. The introduction of enclosure and turnpike gates also made it harder for highwaymen to escape after a robbery. These factors made committing highway robbery less attractive.
- There was an increase in the level of organised crime in this period due to a growth of organised criminal gangs. In the early 18th century, there was an increase in poaching gangs, groups of poachers who joined together to hunt large numbers of animals so they could sell them. Similarly, some smugglers took advantage of the demand for smuggled goods by forming gangs, such as the Hawkhurst Gang, so that they could carry out large-scale smuggling operations.

3 This question is level marked. You should look at the level descriptions on page 90 to help you mark your answer. Here are some points your answer may include:

- The government had a big influence on how minor crimes were punished through its role in the development of the Bloody Code. For example, the government introduced the Waltham Black Act in 1723, which introduced the death penalty for around fifty minor crimes. This change to the law was made because Members of Parliament, who had gained more political power after the English Bill of Rights was passed in 1689, wanted to protect their property. Therefore, the government played a significant role in increasing the number of minor crimes that could be punished by death.
- The government had a big influence on how prisons were used as a punishment in the 19th century, because they passed laws to change the function of prisons. The Prison Act of 1839 led to the introduction of the 'separate system' and the construction of prisons like Pentonville, which aimed to punish criminals, but also to reform them. The government was also responsible for passing the Prisons Act of 1865, which focused on making conditions for prisoners worse so that they would be punished more harshly.
- The government had a big influence on changing the way that witchcraft was punished in the late 17th century. The government introduced the 1736 Witchcraft Act, which stated that witchcraft was not real and that people could be punished by a fine or time in prison for pretending to use magic. This meant that people were now punished for pretending to have magical powers, rather than being punished for witchcraft itself.
- Individuals had a big influence on how witchcraft was punished. John Holt, who was Lord Chief Justice from 1689 to 1710, acquitted many people who had been accused of witchcraft because he believed in examining evidence closely. His actions influenced other judges to do the same, and the number of convictions for witchcraft fell. This meant that judges were already punishing people less harshly for witchcraft before the government changed the law in 1736.
- Public protests had a big influence on how the Tolpuddle Martyrs were punished. In the 1830s, the government reversed their decision to punish the Tolpuddle Martyrs for forming a trade union after pressure from the public. The Tolpuddle Martyrs had originally been sentenced to seven years' transportation, but the government pardoned them after two years because the public objected to their treatment through widespread protests, with 100,000 people gathering in support of the Martyrs at Copenhagen Fields in 1834.
- The attitudes of juries had an impact on the abolition of the Bloody Code. Juries were reluctant to convict petty criminals if it meant they would be executed. This caused some crimes to go unpunished and led to a decline in the use of execution.

4 This question is level marked. You should look at the level descriptions on page 90 to help you mark your answer. Here are some points your answer may include:

- Transportation was more common in the 18th century than it was in the 17th century. Transportation was only possible from 1607 and wasn't commonly used in the 17th century. However, it was used more frequently after 1718, when a law was passed that made it an official alternative to the death penalty.
- Convicts were sent to different places in different periods. American colonies were the only destination for convicts in the 17th century. Although convicts were still sent to America until 1776, the American War of Independence and the establishment of a new colony in Australia meant that all convicts were sent to Australia from 1787.

Answers

- Transportation was used for different purposes in these periods. In the 17th century, transportation was used as a way to commute a death sentence. However, in 1718, transportation became an official alternative to the death penalty, making it a serious punishment in its own right.

5 This question is level marked. You should look at the level descriptions on page 90 to help you mark your answer. Here are some points your answer may include:

- Urbanisation led to changes in policing in towns and cities. After 1750, Britain's population increased dramatically. The urban population grew as many people moved from the countryside to the cities as a result of the Industrial Revolution. The increasing population in cities meant not everyone knew each other, so community policing, which relied on local people taking responsibility for stopping criminals, became less effective. As a result, reforms were made to try and make night watchmen more effective at stopping crimes in urban communities.

- The attempts to reform night watchmen were largely ineffective, and other forms of policing that existed in the mid-18th century were problematic. For example, many thief-takers were thought to be corrupt. Policing in London started to become more professional in the 18th century when important individuals tried to overcome these problems. For example, in 1749, the Fielding brothers set up the Bow Street Runners, an organised group of men who investigated crimes and tried to catch criminals.

- The Bow Street Runners were effective, but they were only a small group, and the need for a more centralised system became clear as London continued to grow. The Home Secretary, Robert Peel, was concerned that there were too many police organisations, which was making policing less effective. As a result, he created the Metropolitan Police Force in 1829 with the aim of making the quality of policing the same across London.

- The creation of the Metropolitan Police led to a greater focus on investigating crimes in London. A detective department of the Metropolitan Police was set up in 1842 to solve crimes. This became the Criminal Investigation Department in 1878.

- The success of the Metropolitan Police led the government to pass the 1856 Police Act, which changed methods of policing in communities across the country. The Act made it compulsory for there to be a police force in all areas. This led to effective and consistent methods of policing being rolled out across the country.

6 This question is level marked. You should look at the level descriptions on page 90 to help you mark your answer. Here are some points your answer may include:

- There was public opposition during this period to the Bloody Code, which made many minor crimes capital offences. For example, the Waltham Black Act, which was passed in 1723, made around fifty minor crimes punishable by death. The Act was seen as extremely harsh by ordinary people, because they thought the punishments didn't match the offences the Act was punishing. Similarly, juries in the early 19th century were often reluctant to convict petty thieves, because they didn't want them to be executed for their crime. This suggests that the public's views on the use of capital punishment for minor crimes didn't change much in this period.

- Although the public's attitude to the use of capital punishment for minor crimes remained the same, the government's attitude changed dramatically. During the early 18th century, the number of minor crimes punishable by death continued to increase, until the death penalty could be given for over 200 minor crimes. This was because the government believed that introducing the death penalty for minor crimes would deter people from damaging property. However, the government's attitude changed when it became clear that the Bloody Code wasn't working as an effective deterrent. The change in the government's attitude is shown by the fact that the Bloody Code was abolished in 1861, ending the use of the death penalty for minor crimes.

- The government's views were partly transformed because of public opposition to the Bloody Code. For example, the reluctance of juries to convict petty thieves meant that some criminals were going unpunished, so crime was actually being encouraged. Therefore, the public's continued opposition to the use of capital punishment had an impact on changing the government's attitude.

- The government's views on the use of capital punishment for minor crimes were also changed because other punishments were seen as suitable alternatives to the death penalty. For example, transportation was used as an official alternative to the death penalty from 1718, while imprisonment became an increasingly common form of punishment in the 19th century.

- Although the government changed its attitude to the use of capital punishment for minor crimes, the death penalty was still seen as an effective punishment for serious crimes. Even after the Bloody Code was abolished in 1861, serious crimes such as murder and treason were still punishable by death. This suggests that the government's views on the effectiveness of the death penalty for punishing serious crimes remained the same.

- Although the government continued to support the use of capital punishment for serious crimes, their views about the most effective way of using capital punishment to deter criminals did change. In the 18th century and early 19th century, it was thought that public execution would demonstrate the power of the state and deter criminals. However, important individuals such as Charles Dickens criticised public executions in the 1840s for lacking a serious atmosphere and actually encouraging crime. This helped to change views on carrying out executions in public, leading to executions being carried out behind closed doors after 1868.

Crime and Punishment in Modern Britain, c.1900-present

Page 55 — Changing Definitions of Crime
Knowledge and Understanding

1 A fine or imprisonment.

2 a) The Irish Republican Army. A group who carried out terrorist attacks in Britain during the Troubles between the late 1960s and 1998.

b) Cyber crime refers to crimes committed using computers and the Internet.

c) The illegal transportation of people across borders.

d) The act of making a crime legal.

3
- Online theft
- Online fraud
- Targeting or disabling other computers
- Copyright theft

4 Criminals are able to commit cyber crimes from far away, often from another country. This makes it hard for police to identify who committed the crime and catch them.

5 The 1967 Abortion Act made it legal to have an abortion with the consent of two doctors.

Thinking Historically

1 a) The smuggling of drugs has become more widespread, and the illegal transportation of people across borders has become an issue.

   b) Certain drugs have become illegal and there has been an increased demand for illegal drugs, meaning people have resorted to smuggling them into the country. Organised gangs have also got involved in people smuggling which has led to it becoming more common.

   c) New types of theft are being committed, for example car theft. Theft is also committed in new ways using computers and the Internet, for example copyright theft.

   d) Developments in technology have created new opportunities for theft. The widespread use of cars has meant the theft of vehicles has become more common. The increased use of technology such as computers and the Internet has created opportunities for theft to be committed online.

2 In the 17th century, James I's response to the Gunpowder Plot was intended to deter others from committing terrorist acts. He did this by punishing the plotters harshly. They were hung, drawn and quartered, and their remains were placed in areas where they could be publicly displayed. In contrast, the government in modern Britain has focused more on preventing terrorists from being able to carry out attacks in the first place. For example, the government passed a law after the 2005 London terror attacks that allowed the authorities to place restrictions on people suspected of being involved in terrorism.

3 In the 1960s, homosexuality and abortion were decriminalised as a result of the government's response to changing social attitudes. As attitudes towards abortion and homosexuality changed, members of the public put pressure on the government to change the law, resulting in the decriminalisation of abortion in 1967 and the decriminalisation of homosexual acts between men aged 21 or over in the same year.

Page 57 — Changing Definitions of Crime
Knowledge and Understanding

1
- Late 1940s — Many immigrants begin to arrive in Britain, including black and Asian immigrants who face hostility from parts of the press and society. This leads to racial tensions in Britain.
- 1958 — West Indian immigrants living in Notting Hill are attacked because of their ethnicity during race riots.
- 1965 — The Race Relations Act is passed. This makes it a crime to discriminate against somebody because of their race or to promote race-related hatred. However, landlords and employers are still able to discriminate based on race.
- 1968 — A new Race Relations Act is passed. This makes it illegal to refuse people housing, employment or public services because of their race.

- 1976 — A third Race Relations Act is passed to replace the first two. This makes indirect discrimination illegal. A Commission for Racial Equality is also set up to ensure this new law is applied.

2 a) It became illegal to discriminate based on gender.

   b) It became illegal to discriminate based on disability.

   c) The Equality Act was brought in which prevented discrimination or harassment based on nine 'protected characteristics', such as age, sexuality and race.

3
- It banned the possession, sale or manufacture of 'controlled' drugs.
- It created three classes of drugs with different penalties for offences involving drugs from each class.

4 The belief that drug use is a victimless crime means that people are less likely to report those who use or sell drugs, making it harder to police drug crime.

Thinking Historically

1 a) The widespread use of cars has led to car theft becoming a crime. It has also led to the creation of driving offences. such as driving faster than the speed limit and driving while under the influence of alcohol or drugs.

   b) New crimes have been created because of the development of mobile phones. For example, in 2003 it became an offence to use a mobile phone while driving.

2 You can choose any of the factors, as long as you explain your answer. For example:
Advances in technology have been the most significant factor. Although the government introduced laws against racial discrimination in response to negative attitudes towards immigrants, advances in technology have had a greater impact on definitions of crime overall, because they have led to the creation of new categories of crime. For example, the invention of cars has led to driving offences being created, while the invention of computers led to the development of cyber crime. Advances in technology have also created new opportunities to commit old crimes. For example, new kings of theft, such as car theft and copyright theft, are now possible. This has forced the government to create new laws to tackle new offences.

Page 59 — Case Study: Conscientious Objectors
Knowledge and Understanding

1 The Military Service Act introduced conscription in 1916, meaning single men aged 18 to 41 had to serve in the army. It was introduced because, although millions of men volunteered to fight in the war, the government still needed more soldiers. According to the Act, men could avoid military service if their current job was important to the war effort, they were ill, or they were a conscientious objector who was given an exemption by a tribunal.

2 A conscientious objector is someone who refuses to take part in a war due to their beliefs.

3
- Some people had political objections to the war.
- Some people felt it was wrong to take the life of another person.
- Fighting in the war was against some people's religious or moral beliefs.

4 The Central Board for Conscientious Objectors was set up in 1939 to better manage what happened to conscientious objectors and make sure that tribunals were fairer during the Second World War than they had been during the First World War.

Answers

Thinking Historically

1 a) Response in WW1:
- They set up tribunals, a type of court, to judge whether a conscientious objector should be exempted from military service. The tribunals could be very hostile towards conscientious objectors.
- The conscientious objectors who failed to convince a tribunal to exempt them could be sent to prison according to the government's orders. In prison, some conscientious objectors had to carry out hard labour and some even died.
- They sent some conscientious objectors to work on farms or in factories.
- They prevented conscientious objectors from voting until 1926.
- They delayed the release of many conscientious objectors until several months after the war had ended.

Response in WW2:
- They had a more tolerant and respectful attitude towards conscientious objectors.
- They set up a Central Board for Conscientious Objectors to better manage what happened to conscientious objectors and ensure tribunals were fair. The Board included people who supported the objectors.
- They sent some conscientious objectors to prison.

b) Response in WW1:
- They were generally very negative towards conscientious objectors because they saw the their refusal to fight as a sign of cowardice.
- They labelled conscientious objectors 'conchies' and handed them white feathers in the street as a sign of their cowardice.

Response in WW2:
- There were several groups who publicly supported conscientious objectors.
- Some objectors were abused by the public in the street.
- Some employers discriminated against conscientious objectors because of their objections.

c) Response in WW1:
- They set up the Non-Combatant Corps (NCC) so conscientious objectors could participate in non-violent, war-related activities such as road building.
- Soldiers in the army criticised conscientious objectors who joined the NCC for refusing to fight.

Response in WW2:
- They accepted conscientious objectors as non-combatants.

2 You can answer either way, as long as you explain your answer. For example:
The treatment of conscientious objectors did change significantly between the First and Second World Wars. Although there was stigma attached to being a conscientious objector in both wars, the government did a lot more to defend conscientious objectors in the Second World War. For example, a Central Board for Conscientious Objectors was set up to make sure that conscientious objectors weren't treated with hostility by tribunals, as they had been in the First World War. Conscientious objectors in the Second World War were also supported by several groups who defended their interests and ensured that more effort was made to accommodate those who objected to fighting, even if COs could still be sent to prison.

3 Both groups were treated harshly by the government to deter others. In 1834, the government sentenced the Tolpuddle Martyrs to seven years' transportation which was the maximum sentence they could give. Similarly, during World War I the government sent some conscientious objectors to prison where some of them died. However, in both cases the government's treatment of each group changed over time. The government pardoned the Tolpuddle Martyrs after two years of their transportation sentence, and it made tribunals fairer for conscientious objectors during the Second World War.

Page 61 — Changes in Law Enforcement

Knowledge and Understanding

1 a) It encourages local people to work together with the police to keep communities safe. For example, local people can report suspicious behaviour and share information with the police.

   b) They serve as a visible police presence in communities by walking a beat and interacting with the public.

2 In the Anglo-Saxon period, local people were expected to help capture criminals, whereas local people in Britain today are not expected to catch criminals themselves.

3 In 1900, police officers only received basic training. However, in 1947 a National Police College was set up to teach new officers the skills required for their job, and today new officers are trained through the College of Policing. Specialist training is also given to those working in certain units, such as Counter Terrorism Units, so they can deal with specific emergencies.

Thinking Historically

1 a) Scientific and technological advances have had a great impact on how the police operate. Forensics have made it easier to link criminals to crimes because fingerprint evidence and DNA can be used to identify criminals. New forms of transport, such as bicycles, cars, speed boats and helicopters, allow officers to pursue suspects more effectively. Communication technology, such as Morse Code transmitters and two-way radios, have allowed officers to coordinate their activities by remaining in contact with one another. The 999 system means police can easily receive information about crimes over the phone. More recently, the development of computer systems has led to improved record keeping and collaboration between forces. The Police National Computer makes it easier to store and share important information such as DNA records and details of missing persons, while CCTV means police can identify suspects by replaying recordings of a crime scene or suspects. The police now have tear gas and weapons that use electric currents to stun criminals so that they can be arrested.

2 a) • c.1500-c.1700 — Policing was mainly focused on catching criminals, although night watchmen played a role in deterring criminals by watching for crime at night. Constables and thief-takers, focused on finding and arresting criminals.
   • c.1700-c.1900 — Policing still had a strong focus on catching criminals, but the police also played a role in deterring criminals. One of the key principles of the Metropolitan Police, which was set up in 1829, was that effective policing would lead to a lack of crime in the first place, demonstrating the increased focus on deterrence.

Answers

- c.1900-present — There was a much greater focus on crime prevention, especially through the use of community policing.

b) • c.1500-c.1700 — There was no professional police force. Constables and night watchmen operated in their own areas, and thief-takers generally worked for themselves.

- c.1700-c.1900 — Policing became more organised as groups like the Bow Street Runners began to take a coordinated approach to catching criminals. The first government-controlled police force, the Metropolitan Police, was created in 1829, and the 1856 Police Act made a police force compulsory for all areas. This meant that policing was organised centrally by the government. A detective department of the Metropolitan Police was set up in 1842, meaning that police work became more specialised.

- c.1900-present — The police were organised into specialist units, such as Firearms Units and Counter Terrorism Units. The number of local police forces was reduced and different police forces were encouraged to work together to make policing more effective.

c) • c.1500-c.1700 — Every male householder was expected to take a turn as a night watchman, suggesting that there were no special requirements to be able to perform this role. Anyone could take advantage of government rewards for catching criminals by becoming a thief-taker.

- c.1700-c.1900 — The Metropolitan Police force had to follow a set of key principles that influenced how they worked. However, the first officers were poorly-trained.

- c.1900-present — A National Police College was established in 1947 to provide basic training for police officers. Recruits are now trained through the College of Policing.

d) • c.1500-c.1700 — Constables were used to arrest criminals and bring them to court. They were also responsible for leading the hue and cry, which local people had to participate in. Night watchmen patrolled the streets at night to catch criminals and deter people from committing crimes. Thief-takers found and captured criminals in exchange for payment.

- c.1700-c.1900 — The Bow Street Runners, who were a more organised gang of thief-takers, began to operate. After the Metropolitan Police was set up in 1829, policemen patrolled in 'beats' to deter and catch criminals. After 1842, detectives were responsible for solving crimes as part of the detective department of the Metropolitan Police.

- c.1900-present — The Neighbourhood Watch was introduced in 1982 and PCSOs were introduced in 2002 to help police the local community and prevent crimes from taking place. Police began to use more advanced technology to help them catch criminals and prevent crime. For example, the invention of forensics meant that fingerprint evidence, bloodstain pattern analysis and DNA analysis could all be used to catch criminals. New forms of transport and more advanced communication technology allowed police to pursue suspects more effectively, while the introduction of computer systems and CCTV helped police to identify suspects. New weapons and protective equipment were also introduced to help police catch criminals.

3 You can choose any of the periods, as long as you explain your answer. For example:
- The period c.1700-c.1900 had the most significant change in law enforcement because policing became more professional and centralised. During this period, the Bow Street Runners and the Metropolitan Police Force were created. The success of centralised policing led to the 1856 Police Act, which made it compulsory for there to be a police force in all areas. Policing also began to focus more heavily on preventing crime by deterring people from committing crime, instead of simply catching criminals. This focus on preventing crime still exists today with initiatives like the Neighbourhood Watch and PCSOs.

Page 63 — The Death Penalty
Knowledge and Understanding
1 a) • The death penalty was seen as a strong deterrent that convinced others not to commit murder.
- Executing murderers was the only certain way to stop them being a threat to society.
- Imprisoning someone for life was more expensive than executing them.
- Death was the only way for society to get retribution for the most appalling murders.

b) • Murders continued to happen despite the death penalty, suggesting it wasn't a strong deterrent. The threat of the death penalty also had little effect on unplanned killings.
- Execution was seen as uncivilised by many because it went against their religious or moral beliefs.
- Countries that no longer used the death penalty had not seen an increase in murder rates.
- Innocent people could be executed if the legal system made a mistake.

2 In 1908, execution of under 16s was banned, although no one under 18 had been executed since 1889.

3 • 1920s — Groups like the Howard League and the National Council for the Abolition of the Death Penalty begin to campaign against capital punishment being used in Britain.
- 1930s — Politicians try to suspend capital punishment, but there isn't enough support in Parliament. However, the execution of pregnant women and people under 18 is banned in the early 1930s.
- 1949 — A Royal Commission is set up to look into whether laws about capital punishment should be changed.
- 1950 — Timothy Evans is hanged after being convicted of killing his wife and child, despite claiming that another man named John Christie was the killer.
- 1953 — The Royal Commission recommends changing the law to remove the death penalty for those who are under 21 and those who have mental health conditions. Evidence emerges that John Christie was the real murderer of Timothy Evans' wife and child, as Evans had claimed. Derek Bentley is executed for the murder of a policeman despite not firing the gun.
- 1955 — Ruth Ellis is hanged for killing her abusive boyfriend. There is a lot of negative press coverage of the execution and public sympathy for Ruth Ellis.
- 1957 — The Homicide Act is passed which introduces different punishments for different categories of murder. This means only the worst kinds of murders are punishable by execution.

Answers

- 1965 — MPs pass the Murder (Abolition of Death Penalty) Act which suspends capital punishment in Britain.
- 1969 — The death penalty is permanently abolished.

Thinking Historically

1 In the 16th century and early 17th century, the government considered that only serious crimes such as murder and treason should be punishable by death. However, from the end of the 17th century onwards, the government began to make many minor offences against property capital crimes under the Bloody Code. This was mainly because many members of the government were landowners, so they wanted to deter people from damaging property. However, the use of execution for crimes against property gradually declined in the early 19th century and it became clear that the Bloody Code was not fit for purpose, leading the government to abolish the death penalty for minor crimes in 1861. In the 1920s, abolitionists began campaigning for an end to execution as a punishment, which encouraged the government to debate the issue. From the end of the 19th century to the 1960s, the government increasingly took action to limit the use of the death penalty, until it was eventually abolished in the 1960s.

2 a) • The government was the driving force in the abolitionist movement, even when public opinion was in favour of keeping the death penalty. Some politicians tried to get capital punishment suspended in the 1930s, but there wasn't enough support for it in Parliament. However, politicians did manage to get the execution of pregnant women and people under 18 banned in the early 1930s. The government also set up a Royal Commission which contributed to removing the death penalty for those under 21 and those who had mental health conditions.
- Some politicians slowed the abolitionist movement down. For example, although MPs voted to suspend the death penalty in 1948, the House of Lords didn't support this idea so it wasn't carried out.

b) • Public attitudes towards capital punishment slowed down the progress of the abolitionist movement. For example, many MPs voted against a move to suspend capital punishment in 1930 because they thought that the public supported capital punishment.

c) • In the 1920s, abolition groups began campaigning to end capital punishment. This caused politicians to discuss the abolition of capital punishment and brought the issue to the public's attention.

3 Those in favour of abolition faced strong opposition. Members of the public continued to support the death penalty, even when it was abolished in the 1960s. This made it difficult for politicians in favour of abolition to get capital punishment suspended in the 1930s and beyond, because other politicians were influenced by public opinion. The use of capital punishment also wasn't considered an important social issue during the 1930s, which delayed its abolition.

Page 65 — Case Study: The Derek Bentley Case

Knowledge and Understanding

1 a) The police arrive and corner Bentley and Craig on the roof. Bentley is detained by DS Fairfax. According to the statements of three policemen, Bentley shouted 'Let him have it, Chris'.

b) More police officers arrive and Craig continues to shoot at them. During the shooting, PC Sidney Miles is killed.

c) Bentley is found guilty and sentenced to death. An appeal to change the decision is unsuccessful, and Bentley is hanged in January 1953.

2 The trial of Bentley and Craig focused on the phrase 'Let him have it'. Bentley was alleged to have said this phrase before Craig started to shoot at DS Fairfax. Those accusing Bentley and Craig of murder suggested that the phrase showed 'common purpose' which meant that they both wanted to kill PC Sidney Miles. However, the lawyers defending Bentley argued he had meant 'Give him the gun'.

3 a) He refused to recommend that the Queen use her 'royal prerogative of mercy' to allow Bentley to go to prison instead of being executed, because he felt there was no reason to do so.

b) 200 MPs signed a petition calling for Bentley to be reprieved.

c) They made pleas for Bentley's life in the media. After his execution, Bentley's family started a campaign to clear his name.

d) Some members of the public sent protests to their MP or rang the Home Office to plead for mercy on Bentley's behalf. Supporters gathered around Parliament and the prison Bentley was held in.

Thinking Historically

1 • High profile cases meant that more people supported the abolitionist movement, because the cases caused many people to question the existing laws about capital punishment. For example, Derek Bentley's case showed that the justice system was open to abuse because it was believed that the death penalty was being misused to make an example of Bentley. This caused support for abolition to grow. The 1957 Homicide Act, which further restricted the use of the death penalty, was partly a response to these cases.
- The media played an important role in raising awareness about many of the issues linked to the death penalty. In the Derek Bentley case, for example, the media was responsible for interviewing members of Derek's family and broadcasting the public protests against his execution. This had the effect of bringing the case to the public's attention.

Page 67 — The Modern Prison System

Knowledge and Understanding

1 a) A parliamentary committee that published a report recommending that British prisons should try to reform offenders, as well as deterring them from committing crimes.

b) A process where an offender meets their victims so they can see the impact of their crimes.

c) A type of school that child offenders could be sent to instead of prison from the 1850s.

d) A type of youth detention centre that first opened in 1902.

e) A type of prison designed to help prisoners prepare for reintegration into society. Inmates are allowed to work outside the prison and can use their leisure time freely.

2 Probation:
- It was officially introduced in 1907.
- As part of the scheme, offenders serve part of their sentence outside of prison.
- The offender has to regularly meet a probation officer who helps them to reform.

Parole:
- It was introduced in 1967.
- It is offered to some offenders after they have served a certain amount of their sentence — this benefits well-behaved offenders, who can leave prison early if they agree to certain conditions.
- It was designed to reduce the number of inmates in prison.
- It helps to rehabilitate prisoners by giving them a chance to reintegrate into society before the end of their sentence.

Community Service Orders:
- They were introduced in 1972.
- They are used for people who have committed their first crime or for those who have committed minor crimes.
- They involve doing community service work, such as getting rid of graffiti or picking up litter.

Thinking Historically

1 a) • Prisons were used to hold people before trial or execution during the 18th century.

b) • During the 19th century, prisons were increasingly used as a punishment in their own right, rather than as a place to hold prisoners before trial. This was partly because the use of transportation was coming to an end by the mid-1850s and the Bloody Code was abolished in 1861, so there were fewer alternatives to prison.
- There was an increased focus on reforming prisoners after the Gaols Act was passed in 1823. This Act introduced measures that aimed to help rehabilitate prisoners, such as letting chaplains visit them. The 'separate system', which was introduced in 1839, was also supposed to help prisoners to reform, for example by allowing them to reflect on their crimes alone.
- There was a focus on using prisons as a deterrent throughout this century. For example, conditions in Pentonville were still harsh, despite this prison being designed with the aim of reforming criminals in mind.
- In the second half of the 19th century there was an increased focus on punishing prisoners, as it became clear that the 'separate system' wasn't working and some people began to believe that it was impossible to reform criminals. The Prisons Act of 1865 made life harsher in prisons so prisoners would suffer for their crime and would be deterred from committing more crimes.

c) • In the early 20th century, there was a renewed focus on reforming prisoners, since the Gladstone Committee recommended that prisons should aim to reform offenders as well as deter them.
- There was an increasing focus on rehabilitating prisoners in the 20th and 21st centuries. Changes to the prison system, such as providing inmates with education and skills, reflected this aim of reforming prisoners. Open prisons were also established in 1933 with the aim of reintegrating prisoners into society.
- Prisons became less focused on punishing prisoners with violence and physical discomfort. Corporal punishments such as flogging and hard labour were abolished in 1948.

2 Here are some points your answer may include:
- Point — There have been significant changes to the way children and young offenders are punished in the period c.1900-present.
- Evidence — The first borstal was opened in 1902, meaning that young offenders aged 16 to 21 were

imprisoned separately from adults for the first time. The age of criminal responsibility was raised in England and Wales during the 20th century from 7 to 8 to 10, and the first juvenile courts were established in 1908.
- Why evidence supports point — The introduction of borstals was a significant development in the way that young offenders are punished because they had been treated in the same way as adults before this. The changes to the law in relation to child offenders built on changes that began in the 1800s, protecting children from being unfairly treated as adults.
- Point — The abolition of the death penalty in the 1960s was a significant change in how criminals were punished.
- Evidence — MPs passed the Murder (Abolition of the death penalty) Act in 1965, which suspended capital punishment in Britain. The death penalty was permanently abolished in 1969. Capital punishment had been used widely as a punishment before the 20th century for crimes such as murder and treason, and it had been used to punish minor crimes under the Bloody Code from the late 17th century to the mid-19th century.
- Why evidence supports point — The abolition of the death penalty meant that criminals could no longer be punished with death. This was significant because the death penalty had been used widely before the 20th century, but now alternative punishments had to be used, even for serious crimes like murder and treason.
- Point — Several alternatives to prison were introduced in the period c.1900-present, representing a significant change in the way criminals are punished.
- Evidence — Probation was introduced in 1907. This means that certain offenders could serve some of their sentence outside of prison. Several alternatives to prison were developed to try to keep people out of prison. These include Community Service Orders, electronic tagging and Criminal Behaviour Orders.
- Why evidence supports point — These alternatives to prison represent a significant change because they reflect the renewed focus on reforming criminals rather than punishing them in the period c.1900-present. Before 1900, there were few forms of punishment that focused so strongly on reforming offenders and preparing them for reintegration into society.
- Point — Despite the focus on reforming prisons, prison continued to be used as a major form of punishment in the period c.1900-present.
- Evidence — Since 1900, the number of inmates in UK prisons has grown significantly. Prison has been used widely as a form of punishment in Britain since the late 1700s.
- Why evidence supports point — Although there are now some alternatives to prison, many criminals are still sent to prison as a punishment. This suggests that the prison has remained an essential method of punishment in modern Britain.
- Point — Some of the changes to the way criminals were punished built on developments that began in the 19th century.
- Evidence — There were changes to the way the death penalty was being used before 1900. For example, the Bloody Code was abolished in 1861, no one under 18 was hanged after 1889.

Answers

- Why evidence supports point — Although the final abolition of the death penalty was a significant change, the process of abolition began in the 19th century when the Bloody Code was abolished, and the use of the death penalty on children had already ended. This suggests that the changes made after 1900 were a continuation of processes that had already begun.

Pages 70 and 71 — Exam-Style Questions

1 This question is level marked. You should look at the level descriptions on page 90 to help you mark your answer. Here are some points your answer may include:
   - In both periods, local people played a role in law enforcement. In the early modern period, local people were expected to join the hue and cry and the 'posse comitatus' to help catch criminals. In the modern period, the Neighbourhood Watch was set up so that local people could work together with the police to keep communities safe by reporting suspicious behaviour.
   - In both periods, law enforcement officers were responsible for catching criminals. In the early modern period, town constables were responsible for arresting criminals. In the modern period, one of the duties of police constables is to arrest criminals.
   - In both periods, local law enforcement involved people patrolling the streets to deter criminals. In the early modern period, night watchmen patrolled the streets at night to deter criminals and look out for crime. In the modern period, PCSOs were introduced to act as a visible police presence in communities. PCSOs patrol in beats and interact with the public to help keep communities safe.

2 This question is level marked. You should look at the level descriptions on page 90 to help you mark your answer. Here are some points your answer may include:
   - Abolitionist groups, such as the Howard League and the National Council for the Abolition of the Death Penalty, were important in prompting the government to debate the abolition of the death penalty. This led to changes in the law in the 1930s so that capital punishment could no longer be used for under 18s and pregnant women.
   - The use of capital punishment changed significantly because government action led to changes in the law. Despite the fact that most of the public were in favour of the death penalty, politicians continued to push for change to the law from the 1930s to the 1960s. In 1969, MPs voted to permanently abolish the death penalty, against the public's wishes. Therefore, the willingness of politicians to ignore public opinion was one of the main reasons why there were changes to the use of capital punishment in this period.
   - Even before the abolition of capital punishment, government action led to changes in the law. In 1949, the government set up a Royal Commission to look into whether laws about capital punishment should be reformed. This led to further changes in the use of the death penalty because in 1953 the Commission recommended that those with mental health conditions and those under 21 should no longer be punished with the death penalty.
   - High profile cases contributed to capital punishment being abolished. For example, in 1953, Derek Bentley was sentenced to death for the murder of a police officer even though he didn't fire the gun that killed the officer.

In the same year, it was discovered that Timothy Evans, who had been hanged in 1950, had been incorrectly sentenced to death. Two years later, Ruth Ellis was hanged, even though she had been abused by her victim. These cases highlighted many of the issues with the death penalty, causing the public and politicians to reconsider the existing laws. This contributed to the introduction of the 1957 Homicide Act, which made only the worst kinds of murders punishable with execution.

3 This question is level marked. You should look at the level descriptions on page 90 to help you mark your answer. Here are some points your answer may include:
   - Changing social attitudes contributed to the decriminalisation of certain crimes in the 20th century. The government's decision to decriminalise both abortion and homosexual acts between men aged 21 and over in 1967 was a response to pressure from members of the public who believed that these actions should no longer be crimes.
   - Although changing social attitudes have led to the decriminalisation of certain acts, other factors have been more important in causing new crimes to be defined. For example, advances in technology have created new types of crime. The widespread ownership of cars in the second half of the 20th century has led to the development of new car-related crimes, such as car theft, drink-driving, speeding and driving while using a mobile phone. Similarly, the invention of computers has led to the development of cyber crime, which includes online theft and fraud, copyright theft and disabling other computers. These new crimes would not have been created without the development of technology.
   - Changes in society have also played an important role in changing definitions of crime. The growth of immigration from the Commonwealth after the Second World War was a key reason why racial discrimination was made a crime in Britain in the modern period. The arrival of many black and Asian immigrants led to a series of race riots in the late 1940s and 1950s, including an attack on West Indian immigrants in Notting Hill in 1958. This led the government to introduce a series of laws to better protect immigrants. For example, the 1965 Race Relations Act made it a crime to discriminate against somebody because of their race.
   - The increased use of drugs in the UK is another change in society that has led to the development of new crimes. The increased use of amphetamines, LSD and cannabis in the 1960s prompted the government to put controls on many drugs, making it illegal to possess substances like amphetamines and LSD. The 1971 Misuse of Drugs Act banned the possession, sale or manufacture of any 'controlled' drugs. This government action was driven by the growing use of drugs in society, rather than a change in social attitudes.

4 This question is level marked. You should look at the level descriptions on page 90 to help you mark your answer. Here are some points your answer may include:
   - The key purpose of punishment was different in each period. In the early modern period, the main purpose of punishment was to deter people from committing crimes. As a result, people guilty of committing minor crimes were punished publicly by being put in the stocks or flogged to humiliate them, so the consequences of crime were visible. In comparison, punishments for minor

crimes in the modern period are designed to help the offender by rehabilitating them and keeping them out of prison. For example, punishments such as Community Service Orders and electronic tagging are supposed to encourage criminals to change their lifestyle so that they won't commit more crimes.

- The death penalty was used for different reasons in these periods. Under the Bloody Code, which began to develop in the late 1600s, the death penalty was used to deter minor property crimes. In contrast, in the first half of the 20th century, the death penalty was used to specifically deter people from committing murder.

5 This question is level marked. You should look at the level descriptions on page 90 to help you mark your answer. Here are some points your answer may include:

- Highway robbery became common in the 18th century because people often travelled long distances in their carriages on rural roads between towns. They often carried valuables with them because of the limited banking system at the time. As a result, they were an attractive target for highway robbers, who attacked travellers and threatened them into giving up their items.
- Highway robbery declined in the 1830s as a result of developments in transport and banking. Enclosure and the introduction of road patrols and turnpike gates made highway robbery less attractive, because it was more difficult for highway robbers to escape. In addition to this, the increase in the use of banknotes at this time made it easier to trace stolen money, further deterring highway robbers.
- Advances in technology have created new opportunities for theft. For example, the invention and widespread use of cars has resulted in the crime of car theft. The development of the Internet has also led to the crime of copyright theft, a type of online theft that involves downloading copyrighted material illegally. This offence is often seen as a social crime, highlighting how attitudes towards theft have also been affected by the invention of the computer and the Internet.
- Advances in technology have also changed the way that theft is carried out. The invention of computers and the Internet means that criminals can carry out fraud and theft online, so they no longer need to be face-to-face with their victim.
- An increase in drug use in the 20th century has led to the growth of drug-related theft. People who are addicted to illegal drugs like heroin and cocaine sometimes steal money to buy drugs.

6 This question is level marked. You should look at the level descriptions on page 90 to help you mark your answer. Here are some points your answer may include:

- Individuals played an important role in the development of policing in the 18th century. The Fielding brothers were responsible for creating the Bow Street Runners in 1749. The Bow Street Runners have been described as the first professional police force in Britain. They played a key role in coordinating and improving national policing. For example, they published a newsletter called the *Hue and Cry* that described wanted criminals, making them easier to capture.
- Individuals continued to play an important role in the early 19th century. Robert Peel was particularly important in the development of policing. After the success of the Bow Street Runners, he created the Metropolitan Police Force in 1829. This was because he saw the need for a coordinated, government-controlled policing service to replace the many different police organisations that had been operating in the 18th century. The success of Peel's force led to the 1856 Police Act, which made a police force compulsory for all areas. The principles of Peel's Metropolitan Police Force are still in use today, showing the influence he has had on the development of policing.

- Since the turn of the 20th century, other factors have been more important in the development of policing. In the 20th century, advances in technology influenced the way the police operated. For example, police started to use Morse Code transmitters in the 1920s and two-way radios in the 1930s. These inventions allowed police officers to better coordinate their activities. This has made the police more effective at catching criminals.
- Scientific advances in the 20th century have also helped to develop policing. The police began using forensics in the early 20th century, meaning that they could catch criminals by matching their fingerprints or DNA to the crime scene. This means the police are able to solve crimes in new ways.
- Improvements in police training in the 20th century have contributed to the development of policing. Before 1900, police officers received basic training. However, in 1947, the National Police College was set up to teach recruits the skills they need to carry out the role effectively. Specialist units, such as Firearms Units and Counter Terrorism Units, have also been developed. These changes have improved the quality of police officers, making them more effective.
- Structural changes to the police force since 1900 have also helped to develop policing. The number of local police forces has been reduced since 1900 to 43. Records are also now stored centrally, which has meant police forces can share information. These developments have made it easier for police forces to work together more effectively.

Whitechapel, c.1870-c.1900

Page 73 — Housing and Employment
Knowledge and Understanding

1 a) An overcrowded slum that had narrow, winding streets and low-quality housing in unstable buildings that could be several storeys high.

b) A type of lodging house where lodgers could sleep on bunk beds for just a few pence a night. Lodgers could sleep upright and leaning over a rope for even less money.

c) A type of free accommodation for young, old, poor and ill people, who would otherwise be homeless. The accommodation was generally unpleasant, discipline was harsh and families could be split up. People staying in workhouses were often made to work long hours in return for accommodation.

2 The construction of the Peabody Estate improved housing conditions in one small area, but made the overcrowding problem in Whitechapel as a whole worse. This is because the rent was higher in the new Estate and many families were unable to afford it. As a result, these families had to move away from the Peabody Estate and find accommodation in other parts of Whitechapel.

Answers

3   • Lack of permanent lodgings — Many people were forced to move between lodging houses or live in workhouses because they didn't have a regular income to pay rent with.
    • Health issues — Diseases like diphtheria and dysentery spread easily due to overcrowding. The high levels of poverty meant that people struggled to recover from these illnesses because they couldn't afford to feed themselves properly.
    • Crime — The high levels of poverty and unemployment meant that people were desperate for money so often turned to crime as a way of making money.
    • Prostitution — The lack of jobs meant that many women were forced to become prostitutes in order to survive.
    • Discontent and desperation — The problems caused by poverty and the difficulty of finding work meant that many people in Whitechapel were frustrated and unhappy.

Source Analysis

1 b) How many people lived in Whitechapel's lodging houses in around 1870?
   c) What was it like to stay in a lodging house in Whitechapel in 1870?
   d) Was disease more common in lodging houses than in other types of Whitechapel accommodation?

2 a) Police records that show the lodging houses registered with the police in different areas of London — This would allow me to compare the number of lodging houses in Whitechapel to the number in other parts of London, to see if there was a big difference.
   b) Census records for Whitechapel from 1871 that show the occupants of each lodging house in Whitechapel. — This would allow me to work out the number of people in Whitechapel who lived in lodging houses shortly after 1870.
   c) First-hand accounts of conditions in lodging houses in Whitechapel from Charles Booth's social survey of London — Booth's descriptions of the conditions inside a lodging house would reveal the problems that lodging house residents faced in the late 19th century.
   d) A medical report from the Medical Officer of Whitechapel that shows how many patients were sent to London hospitals from each type of Whitechapel dwelling. — This would allow me to work out whether more lodging house residents were suffering from certain diseases than people who lived in workhouses or other types of dwelling.

Page 75 — Social Tensions

Source Analysis

1 b) The source is useful because it was drawn by an illustrator for the *English Illustrated Magazine* who might have been trying to capture public opinion in his cartoon. This means that the source is likely to represent a typical view of Jewish traders held by the magazine's readers. The usefulness of the source is limited because it's not possible to tell how far the author has reflected public opinion and how far he has reflected his own personal views.
   c) The usefulness of this source is limited because the Jewish trader in the cartoon is presented in an unrealistic way, suggesting that the cartoon is designed to give an exaggeratedly negative view of Jewish traders. The cartoon therefore might not accurately reflect the strength of people's negative attitudes towards Jewish traders.

2 a) The source is useful because it shows that Booth held the prejudiced belief that Jewish people were happy living 'on the middle ground between civilization and barbarism'. Booth chose to publish this view in his survey, which suggests that it wasn't controversial among the audience of his survey. It is true that there was a lot of prejudice towards Jews at this time, which supports the idea that Booth's view was typical. The usefulness of the source is limited because it only directly expresses one person's experience of how Jewish immigrants in Whitechapel lived.
   b) The source is useful because its author, Charles Booth, had actually visited Whitechapel as a result of his work as a social reformer and researcher who studied the problem of poverty in London for many years. This means that his views are based on his first-hand experience of Whitechapel, instead of on hearsay.
   c) The usefulness of the source for this investigation is limited because it was designed to be a scientific study of poverty in London, so Booth wasn't necessarily interested in people's attitudes towards Jewish immigrants. Therefore, his view is unlikely to be based on research into the lives of Jewish immigrants or conversations he had with them.

Knowledge and Understanding

1   The constant movement of people around Whitechapel made it easier for people to commit crimes. This is because people were unlikely to know their neighbours well, meaning they were less likely to look out for each other. Theft was also common because lodgers had to carry all their possessions with them, making them easy targets. It was hard for the police to catch criminals because suspects and witnesses would often move from place to place so it was difficult for police to properly investigate crimes and find the perpetrators.

2 a) Many people believed immigrants were taking jobs away from them, because many Jewish immigrants were willing to work long hours for little money in sweatshops.
   b) People blamed immigrants for overcrowding because there was an increase in Irish and Jewish immigrants coming to Whitechapel and renting accommodation there.
   c) Immigrants were often blamed for crime because some of the violent gangs in Whitechapel were made up of newly arrived immigrants.
   d) People blamed Jewish immigrants for the rise in support for socialism and anarchism because many Jewish immigrants were familiar with these ideas, which had originated in Eastern Europe. This association between Jewish people in Whitechapel and radical beliefs was strengthened by the fact that some Jewish immigrants set up socialist organisations and newspapers.

Page 77 — Policing in the Late 19th Century

Knowledge and Understanding

1 a) Sir Edmund Henderson was Police Commissioner from 1869-1886.
   b) Sir Charles Warren was Police Commissioner from 1886-1888.
   c) It was set up in the year 1829.
   d) It was split into divisions, which were each responsible for a particular area of London.
   e) It was reorganised in 1878.
   f) Its main role in the Police was to investigate crimes and find out who had committed them.

Answers

Source Analysis

1   Investigation b), because the source shows that the Police Commissioner had to deny that the Police were like soldiers, suggesting that they had been criticised for this.

2   • The source would be less useful for investigation a) because it only shows Charles Warren's reaction to criticisms of the Police, and it doesn't show how policemen in the Metropolitan Police actually felt about these criticisms.
    • The source would be less useful for investigation c) because it only shows criticisms of the Police in 1888, and it doesn't give any details about how many people agreed with these criticisms.

Page 79 — Policing Whitechapel

Source Analysis

1 a) Was it difficult for Whitechapel police constables to carry out their duties at night in the 1870s?
  b) Was it common for the police to patrol in groups rather than on their own in Whitechapel in the 1870s?
  c) What problems did homelessness in Whitechapel cause for police officers in the 1870s?

2 a) The memoirs of a police constable from H Division that describe night patrols — This would give a first-hand account of what it felt like to carry out a night patrol, which might reveal the challenges that officers faced.
  b) Metropolitan Police Records for H Division showing the duties assigned to each police officer — This would show how many policemen in H Division were assigned to each beat so I could work out whether patrolling in groups was typical.
  c) Old Bailey court records for the 1870s giving details of cases involving homeless victims and perpetrators of crime — This would show the types of crimes that were associated with homelessness that the police had to deal with in Whitechapel in the 1870s, and it would also give an idea of how frequently homelessness was a factor in crime.

Knowledge and Understanding

1   • Patrolling in 'beats' allowed H Division to cover the whole of Whitechapel in an organised way, meaning there was no part of the area that was unmonitored.
    • Constables followed the same routes so they could be located quickly if they were needed.

2   The main problem of patrolling in 'beats' was that criminals could learn the route and then work out when they could commit a crime without the police being there.

3 a) • Alcoholism was common in Whitechapel — drinking made people more likely to be involved in a crime, either as the victim or the perpetrator.
    • Prostitution was widespread — prostitutes in Whitechapel were often the victims of attacks by their clients.
    • There were many criminal gangs operating in Whitechapel — these gangs were responsible for lots of different crimes, such as setting up illegal gambling and fights, and violent crime linked to protection rackets.
    • Negative attitudes towards Jewish people meant that violence against Jews was common.
  b) • The nature of Whitechapel's streets made it hard to catch criminals — it was easy for criminals to hide in the narrow, dark alleys of the rookeries.
    • Lots of local people were hostile to the police, making it harder for the police to work with them to stop crime.

• There weren't enough policemen on patrol to stop crime effectively.
• Police constables were only armed with a truncheon, while criminals might have knives or even guns.

Page 81 — Jack the Ripper

Source Analysis

1 a) The source is useful because it was written by the police and is therefore a direct example of how they appealed for information while investigating the Ripper murders.
  b) The source is useful because it was written after four of the Ripper murders had been carried out, so it shows that police were making widespread appeals for information at the height of the Ripper murders. The usefulness of the source is limited because it doesn't show when the police began to use this technique, or whether they continued to use it after the fifth and final murder in November 1888.
  c) The source is useful because its message was specifically aimed at the people of Whitechapel, which shows that police directly targeted the people who were most likely to have seen or witnessed something that might advance the police's investigation.
  d) The source is useful because it shows that the police wanted people to report to a local police station if they suspected anyone of being involved in the Ripper murders. This suggests that the police did not have any suspects at this point in the investigation and were using the technique of asking local residents to offer information that might lead them to a suspect.

Knowledge and Understanding

1   • 31st August 1888 — Mary Ann Nichols's body was discovered on the street. Her body was taken away before police could make a detailed observation of the scene.
    • 8th September 1888 — Annie Chapman's body was discovered on the street.
    • 30th September 1888 — The bodies of Elizabeth Stride and Catherine Eddowes were discovered on the street.
    • 9th November 1888 — Mary Jane Kelly's body was discovered. She was the only victim to be found in her house rather than on the street. Photographs were taken of the room where she was killed.

2 a) Police weren't always able to make a detailed observation of the scene because the Police Code wasn't always followed. For example, the body of Mary Ann Nichols was removed before the inspector arrived.
  b) The information police gathered by interviewing witnesses and suspects didn't lead anywhere and was often made up. They were unable to offer rewards for information in case it encouraged people to make up evidence.
  c) Police sketches were usually drawn in an unrealistic style and so didn't provide very accurate representations of crime scenes.

3   The result of the autopsies led police to believe that the killer was left-handed and that he was someone with a good knowledge of anatomy, such as a butcher.

4   Before the Ripper murders, photography had mainly been used by the Metropolitan Police to identify murder victims, usually after the body had been removed from the crime scene. However, by 1888 the Metropolitan Police were beginning to take photos of crime scenes to record their findings.

Answers

Page 83 — Jack the Ripper

Knowledge and Understanding

1
   - Their failure to cooperate sometimes meant that it was difficult to make important decisions about the case.
   - It caused the police to appear disorganised, so they faced more criticism from the media and the public.

2 a) The public became confused about what had really happened, making it harder for the police to get reliable evidence from members of the public.

   b) The police wasted time dealing with public criticism when they could have been investigating the murders.

3 The Whitechapel Vigilance Committee were a group of local people from Whitechapel who tried to protect the community by patrolling the streets and attempting to solve the Ripper murders themselves. They hired private detectives and offered a reward for information.

Source Analysis

1 a)
   - The source is useful for this investigation because it shows how the media's portrayal of the Ripper murders was often sensationalised. The source claims that the murder of Mary Jane Kelly was the 'seventh' the Ripper had committed, whereas historians now believe there were only four previous murders carried out by the Ripper at this point. Inaccurate claims like this and the sensational language (e.g. 'fiendish') used in the source show how the media's portrayal of the murders made it difficult for people to know the truth.
   - The source is useful because it comes from a leading London newspaper so is likely to show a typical representation of how the Ripper murders were portrayed in the London press.
   - The source is useful because it was written just after the last of Jack the Ripper's murders, so it shows how the media portrayed the murder of Mary Jane Kelly specifically but also the Ripper case as a whole.

   b)
   - The usefulness of the source is limited because it doesn't show how the murders were presented in other areas of the media, such as opinion pieces and satirical cartoons published in magazines and newspapers.
   - The usefulness of the source is limited because it was written directly after the last murder, so it doesn't show how the media portrayed the first murders when they happened, or whether the media's portrayal of the murders changed as time went on.

Page 85 — Types of Sources

Source Analysis

1 a)
   - Examples — official records, government reports, surveys, letters, first-hand accounts (diaries, memoirs, witness statements, first-hand reports)
   - Some documents (e.g. government reports) can be useful if you're looking for factual information about a historical site or the people who used it. There's often a date attached, which is useful if you're looking for evidence from a specific point in a site's history. Other documents (e.g. official records) can be useful for spotting patterns or working out how typical a piece of evidence is. First-hand accounts can give a good understanding of what a historical site was like.
   - It's sometimes hard to judge how reliable the facts in documents are. This is because they're usually quite one-sided, and it's not always clear who wrote them. First-hand accounts aren't always useful for finding out

specific facts because they often focus on one person's personal experience.

   b)
   - Examples — Local newspaper articles, national newspaper articles, magazine articles, opinion pieces
   - Newspaper articles can be useful if you want to find out about public opinion about a historical site. They can also show how events were presented to the public.
   - Newspaper articles didn't always report the truth and often expressed exaggerated or sensational views to try to attract a reader's attention. They usually reflect the author's views, so can be quite one-sided.

   c)
   - Examples — photographs, maps, illustrations, cartoons
   - Some image sources can be useful for understanding what a site looked like or where different things were located. Some image sources such as *Punch* illustrations are useful for revealing the issues that journalists and their readers were concerned about.
   - Maps and diagrams don't show what it was like to live in a historical site or what people thought about life there. Photographs only show what the photographer chose to focus on, and illustrations may be biased towards the illustrator's opinion.

2 a) How often did Whitechapel police have to deal with violent crime in the 1880s?

   b) Was it safer to be a police officer in Whitechapel in 1888 than in 1870?

   c) Did H Division constables patrol Thrawl Street in pairs?

3 a) Old Bailey records of criminal trials related to the Whitechapel area in the 1880s — The testimonies of criminals and policemen in cases involving violent crime would allow me to see how often police had to deal with violent crime as it happened.

   b) Metropolitan Police records listing the cause of death of police constables in H Division — These records would allow me to see whether the number of police constables who died during their work decreased between 1870 and 1888. They would also contain information about the cause of death, so I would be able to see how many (if any) of the deaths were caused by active service.

   c) Police records from H Division showing police officers assigned to cover the beat that included Thrawl Street. — This would allow me to work out whether it was common practice to assign two officers to patrol Thrawl Street.

4 The usefulness of the source is limited because the article's title, 'An Autumn Evening in Whitechapel', suggests that the purpose of the article was to give the magazine's readers an exciting and sensational view of an evening in Whitechapel. This means that the suggestion that theft is common might be exaggerated. The usefulness of the source is further limited by the fact that it comes from an American magazine, as it is possible that the author has not actually visited Whitechapel, or is painting a particularly sensational picture for their American readers.

5 The source was written in 1888 at the height of the Ripper murders. This limits its usefulness as an accurate representation of the reasons why crime was common in Whitechapel, as the killings caused the media and the general public to develop a great interest in Whitechapel that may have encouraged journalists to exaggerate the negative features of life in Whitechapel and the reasons for crime there.

Answers

Pages 88-89 — Exam-Style Questions

1 Each feature is marked separately and you can have a maximum of two marks per feature. How to grade your answer:
- 1 mark for describing one credible feature of the local population in Whitechapel.
- 2 marks for describing one feature and for giving some supporting information that provides more detail.

Here are some points your answer may include:
- The local population in Whitechapel was constantly changing. Lots of people lived in lodging houses, workhouses or on the streets just for one or two nights.
- The population of Whitechapel was typically very poor. Many worked in low-paid jobs or were unemployed.
- There was a high number of immigrants in Whitechapel. Many Irish and Jewish people settled there in the late 19th century.
- The local population in Whitechapel often lived in low-quality housing with poor sanitation, which meant disease was common among the population.
- Some people in Whitechapel became criminals. Poverty made some people so desperate they resorted to crime.
- Some of the population in Whitechapel were part of gangs. Gang members used protection rackets to make money.
- Many people in Whitechapel were addicted to alcohol. Alcohol addiction made some people in Whitechapel more likely to commit crime or be a victim of crime.

2 This question is level marked. How to grade your answer:

Level 1 1-2 marks	The answer gives a simple analysis of the sources to come to a basic judgement about their usefulness for the investigation. It shows a basic understanding of the sources' content and/or provenance, as well as displaying some relevant knowledge of the topic.
Level 2 3-5 marks	The answer analyses the sources in more detail to make judgements about their usefulness for the investigation. It shows a good understanding of the sources' content and/or provenance and uses relevant knowledge to support its judgements.
Level 3 6-8 marks	The answer evaluates the sources to make judgements about their usefulness for the investigation. It shows a detailed understanding of the sources and uses relevant knowledge to analyse their content and provenance, and to support its judgements.

Here are some points your answer may include:
- Source A is useful because it suggests that the media caused the police issues by revealing their movements to the public. There was a lot of media speculation in 1888 about the Ripper murders and this resulted in lots of false evidence, giving support to the source's suggestion that the media caused the Ripper detectives problems.
- Source A is useful because it was published in October 1888, after the first four Ripper murders. It shows that the issues caused by media reporting of the Ripper case were recognised by members of the media at the time, suggesting that they were a legitimate concern.
- The usefulness of Source A is limited because it is not designed to give a realistic depiction of the impact of media reporting. The clown-like appearance of the reporter suggests that the cartoon is designed to create

humour for readers of *Punch*, as well as to make a point, so it may be exaggerating how negative the effects of media reporting were for the police.
- Source A does not show the thoughts of the detectives on the Ripper case, so it is not useful for discovering how far the police felt hampered by media reporting.
- Source B is useful because it shows that Charles Warren, who was in charge of the Metropolitan Police and closely involved in the Ripper case, read and replied to a letter published in the media. This will have taken time, suggesting that the media might have distracted the police's leader from focusing on the case.
- Source B is useful because it is from 1888 and therefore shows that the police were being criticised by the public while they were investigating the murders. This reflects the way that media reporting increased the pressure that the police were under in 1888 to catch the Ripper.
- Source B is useful because it shows how people outside the investigation didn't always understand the context of the Ripper murders, e.g. the fact that people had been 'walking all evening' along Whitechapel's streets and how this could reduce the effectiveness of bloodhounds. This indicates that the media reporting of the Ripper murders caused issues by confusing the public's understanding of the case.
- Source B is useful because it is from Charles Warren himself in his role as Police Commissioner, which shows that a leader of the police felt troubled enough by media reporting of the Ripper case that he decided to respond.
- The usefulness of Source B is limited because it only concerns Percy Lindley's letter and doesn't show whether police detectives were paying attention to other things published in the media. It's not possible to tell from the source whether the police had to respond to other instances of media reporting.
- The usefulness of Source B is limited because it only shows Charles Warren's response to Percy Lindley. It does not show the contents of Lindley's letter or how the media presented it, so it is not possible to judge how this reporting might have affected the police investigation.

3 Each bullet point is marked separately and you can have a maximum of one mark per bullet point. How to grade your answer:
- 1 mark for giving a detail from Source A that you could investigate.
- 1 mark for giving a question to investigate the detail from Source A.
- 1 mark for suggesting an appropriate source to use.
- 1 mark for explaining how the source could help to answer your follow-up question.

Here is an example answer you could give:
- Detail from Source A to investigate: The suggestion in the cartoon that the police detective doesn't want the reporter to shine their light on them.
- Question you would ask: Did detectives find media attention to be disruptive during the Jack the Ripper case?
- The type of source you might use: Memoirs written by detectives who had worked on the Ripper case.
- How this could help answer the question: The memoirs might show how the Ripper detectives felt about the media attention the case received.

Index

HECPO41